Crumbs From
The Master's Table

Nourishment for the Followers of Christ

Cherrie Plowden Jordan

Under the inspiration of the Holy Spirit
Matthew 15:26–28

Kendrick, Alex & Max,

To God be the glory!

Cherrie P. Jordan

Love in Christ!

Isaiah 40:31

Strategic Book Group

Strategic Book Group
P.O. Box 333
Durham, CT 06422

www.StrategicBookClub.com

ISBN: 978-1-61204-147-6

I dedicate this book to my Grandpapa Steadman S. Jackson (1870–1952). He taught me about Jesus: who He is, what He did for me, and why I should love and fear Him. Without Grandpapa and his teaching, I might never have become a Christian.

"You did not choose Me, but I chose you, and appointed you, that you should go and bear fruit, and that your fruit should remain, that whatever you ask of the Father in My name, He may give to you."

John 15:16 (NAS)

Contents

Acknowledgments xi

Introduction: My Grandpapa xiii

A Praline 1

A Psalm For Thanksgiving 3

A Sinner-Seeking Church. 5

A Song Of Praise 7

Aid And Comfort. 11

Are You Washed? 13

Beauty Of Holiness 15

Being Thankful In Our Catastrophe. 17

Bow Of Promise. 19

Do I Really Care?. 21

Don't Leave The Lord Jesus At Church. 23

Don't Let The Door Shut You Out! 25

Faith For Today 29

Feathers Of Blessings 31

Feed The Flock. 33

From Riches To Rags 35

God Heals 37

God Sings! 39

God's Eternal Power 41

God's Mission For Us. 43

He Rolled Away The Stone. 45

Hear And Do. 47

His Own 49

I Did It. 51

I Trust You, Father 53

I've Just Seen Jesus 55
John 17: The Real Lord's Prayer 57
"Joint Heirs". 61
Keep Your Eyes On The Prize. 63
Know His Voice 65
Let's Go Fishing 67
Light In The Forest 69
Looking At The Lamb 71
Looking Up 73
Magnificent Presence 75
My Friend 79
My Tribute To Sara. 81
No Ram 83
Nothing But The Blood 85
The Cabin 87
Our Constant Lord 89
Outside The Gate. 91
Reject Him? Not Me, Lord! 93
Set Free 95
Sin's Price. 97
Stairway 99
Tears On My Feet. 101
The Answer 103
The Butterfly 105
The Cross. 107
The Eyes Of God 109
The Gift That Gives. 111
The Light And The Lamp 115
The Mourning, Morning Star 117
The One Who Spoke 119
The Real Meaning Of Easter 121
The Reply 123
The Sweetest Words 125

Wash His Feet 127
What A Savior!. 129
Who Is This Baby? 131
Who Knows Better? 133
Crumbles 135

Acknowledgments

Thank you to my daughter, Wendi Jordan Wooddell, for spending time editing and advising me to make my words work.

Also, thank you to my very dear friend and neighbor, Loretta Emory, for the many hours spent typing and editing my manuscript on her computer.

Thanks to my aunt, Sue Hyer, for believing in me and giving me the opportunity to have my work published. She has now gone home to be with our Lord.

Thanks to my special friend, Judy Enos, who put many hours into editing my book.

Introduction

MY GRANDPAPA

My grandpapa was a very special person to me. Only God knows how special and what a profound effect he had and still has on me to this day. Grandpapa loved Jesus and showed it. He wanted everyone he knew to make Jesus "Lord" of their lives.

Grandpapa was a humble man, not formally educated. I think he went as far as the fourth grade in school; however, he was wise, kind, loving, slow to anger, and quick to forgive.

My earliest memory of him was when I was about four years old, and we (my mother, daddy, and baby brother) moved in with him and Grandmama. Their home was a large two-story farmhouse with big rooms, including five bedrooms—plenty of room for the four of us. I grew up in their big house, which was full of love, and didn't leave until I was married.

Grandpapa loved each of his seven children and twenty grandchildren. However, I always felt that I was the most blessed of them because I was the one who "lived" with him! He loved me with the most unconditional love ever, and that's the way I loved him back.

Grandpapa also taught me to pray. He was the greatest praying man I have ever known. He and Grandmama went to bed early almost every night because they got up early. I could hear him praying each evening as I went up the stairs to my room, which was directly above theirs. I could hear the gentle hum of his voice as he talked to God. He always knelt by his bed to pray.

Grandpapa had been blind with cataracts since he was in his fifties, but I never in my life with him heard him complain. Furthermore, he was interested in anything about me, and I took everything I bought to him so he could "see" it. So many wonderful memories I have in my heart about my time with him.

Grandpapa has been with Jesus since 1952. For me, his legacy is the prayers he prayed for me. I can still feel those prayers around me today and miss him terribly.

As you read this book, I hope it is a time of worship and meditation for you. Take your time to look up the Scriptures and to reflect on what God wants you to learn and know. After you have read and absorbed His "food" for you, your appetite for His "bread of life" will never fade.

A crumb from His table: Thanks, Grandpapa for loving me and telling me about Jesus.

I love you,

Cherrie Hope

A Praline

SCRIPTURE: PHILIPPIANS 4:18 (KJB)

*"An odour of a sweet smell, a sacrifice acceptable,
well pleasing to God."*

Do you like pralines? Taste how good they are on your tongue! The sweetness of the candy and the texture of the pecans, giving off their wonderful nutty flavor, is a delicious experience to our senses.

First, we see them. Right away we begin to want one. Second, we feel it as we pick one up. Third, we smell it as we raise it to our lips. Fourth, taste the mouth-watering first bite. Fifth, we hear its pleasant sound as we crush it between our teeth. This is a mouth-watering experience, isn't it?

Can you think about your life experience with Jesus as you think about the praline? First, we see Him. When we learn who and what He is, we want Him. Second, we begin to feel who He is as we learn more about Him. Third, we begin to smell His sweet aroma as we lose ourselves in Him. Fourth, as we taste the sweetness of His words and love for us, we love Him more and more. Fifth, we hear the pleasant sound of our praises to Him in song and prayer, which is a sweet aroma to Him. Now, can you see Jesus in a praline? One "bite" leads to many more.

A CRUMB FROM HIS TABLE: LORD, HELP ME TO EXPERIENCE YOU IN EVERYTHING I SEE, FEEL, SMELL, TASTE, AND HEAR.

A Psalm For Thanksgiving

SCRIPTURE: PSALM 100 (NKJV)

The theme of this Psalm is God's goodness and evidence of His love and faithfulness.

The psalmist begins the hymn with an invitation to the whole earth to join the chorus of voices praising our God. It is especially meant for the believers, but it is offered to "all ye lands."

We, as worshipers, are challenged to "serve the Lord with gladness." Don't come into His presence with a "grouch" on. Be joyful! Be glad! Sing! Show those unsaved how happy Christ Followers are! We serve a Mighty God! We praise the Son and the Holy Spirit and have everything in which to be thankful (Ephesians 5:20 NAS).

We, Followers, know who God is. He is our Heavenly Father. But He is not so far away from us. We know He is as close as our next breath. It is God who made us. We certainly cannot make ourselves. There is no such thing as a "self-made man." We belong to Him. One of the most loved sayings is, "We like sheep." We are the "sheep of His pasture." We are HIS people!

Again, the psalmist invites the worshipers to enter the gates of God's sanctuary, giving Him thanks. "Enter His gates with

3

thanksgiving." We are to come into the special place He has created just for the purpose of praising Him with song and confession. We cannot worship Him in truth until we have confessed our sin to Him, (Romans 10:9–10). We end our confession with our blessing His Holy Name: YAHWEH (GOD.)

We sing our praises to Him, again. We give thanks for His eternal love and sacrifice for us. Oh Lord, may we never forget Your great love and sacrifice for us. Yes, Lord, we are Yours because You have bought us with an unthinkable price—Your only Son! We praise You for Your goodness, Your loving kindness, and for being our faithful God—not only to us but to all who come after us.

Thanksgiving Day is set aside in our nation to give God thanks. But we, as Christ Followers, have Thanksgiving every day. There are not enough days in our lives for us to thank Him sufficiently. Even on days of hardship and trouble, if we look, we can find something in which to be thankful.

Let us say the 100th Psalm together:

"Make a joyful noise unto the Lord, all you lands.

Serve the Lord with gladness; come before His presence with singing.

Know that the Lord He is God; it is He that has made us, and not we ourselves;

We are His people and the sheep of His pasture.

Enter into His gates with thanksgiving, and into His courts with praise.

Be thankful to Him, and bless His name.

For the Lord is good; His mercy endures to all generations."

CRUMBS FROM HIS TABLE: "IF WE CONFESS OUR SINS, HE IS FAITHFUL AND JUST TO FORGIVE US OUR SINS AND TO CLEANSE US FROM ALL UNRIGHTEOUSNESS," (1 JOHN 1:9 NKJV).

A Sinner-Seeking Church

SCRIPTURE: AMOS 6:1–8 (ASV)

"Woe to them that are at ease in Zion...."

Praise You, O God! Praise You in the morning! Praise You in the evening! "My heart panteth after Thee."

As I opened my Bible, You gave me Amos to read. In Amos 6:1, it says, "Woe to those who are at ease in Zion." Woe to those who are satisfied with the status quo in the church body, who don't seem to see the need of reaching out to the lost ones around them. They feel "secure in the mountain of Samaria." They feel secure and relaxed that they have done their part for the Lord.

Why? Didn't they build beautiful buildings in honor of Christ? It's not their fault that people don't come and be saved! Look over in neighboring areas. Why are people being saved over there? Why are people happy and full of joy there? Why are they worshiping with much joy and enthusiasm? Is their territory greater than yours?

Maybe while you "sprawled on your couches of ivory," ate the "fatted calves," drank the wine offered to idols, and anointed

5

yourselves with fine perfume, you never grieved over the ruin of lost mankind.

God has declared that He loathes their arrogance and will deliver them up to eternal separation from Him. His word is REPENT. Search for Him. Find Him. Join Him. Stay with Him. Follow Him no matter what the world may say. WORSHIP HIM!!! Not self!

CRUMBS FROM HIS TABLE: IN JAMES 5:20, GOD AFFIRMS THAT HE LOVES A SINNER-SEEKING CHURCH!

A Song Of Praise

SCRIPTURE: JOHN 1:14 (NAS)
"And the Word became flesh and dwelt among us..."

A new song we could sing in church could be "There Is No One Like Jesus." This is a song I've made up:

There is no one like Jesus;
No one affects my heart like You.
I search forever for You.
How merciful You are.
Healing in Your hands.
We, Your children, are safe in Your arms.

It is really a song of praise to our Lord Jesus, and it should always come from our spiritual hearts. Let's look at the words and feel what they mean.

First of all, "There is no one like Jesus." The Scripture says, "The Word became flesh and dwelt among us, and we beheld His glory, glory as of the only begotten from the Father, full of grace and truth," (John 1:14 NAS). God who "spoke" the world into existence "spoke" Christ into the world as its Savior. "…for I have not even come on My own initiative, but He sent Me," (John 8:42b NAS). "Truly, truly I say unto you, before Abraham was born, I am," (John 8:58 NAS). Jesus is telling the Jews who He is. "I Am" is the name God called Himself, (Exodus 3:14).

In Matthew 1:18–25, we find the fulfillment of the promises made in the Old Testament in Isaiah 9:6 of the birth of God's Son.

Other Scriptures to prove there is none like Him are: John 1:1, 2, 15—eternal; 2 Corinthians 5:21—sinless; and Revelation 21:6— the beginning of the end.

The second line of the song declares, "No One affects my heart like You." Here, again, we find many verses in God's Word that show how He touches our hearts.

"For He knows the secrets of the heart," (Psalm 44:21 NAS). We cannot hide from God. He knows everything about us to the minutest part of our being. "…for the Lord searches all hearts, and understands every intent of the thoughts," (1 Chronicles 28:9b NAS). If we are well grounded in His Word and trust Him to keep watch over our thoughts, we can be sure that what is in our hearts is pure.

God enlightens our hearts to enable us to see Him in the face of Jesus: "…God said, 'Light up the darkness!' and our lives filled up with light as we saw and understood God in the face of Christ, all bright and beautiful," (2 Corinthians 4:6, The Message Bible).

When we are "tuned" into Christ, it is easier for us to hear His instructions to us. Did you know that you have two kinds of ears? Physical ears and spiritual ears. Our physical ears are always "on." We have to "turn on" our spiritual ears until they become "tuned in" for good. That means our physical ears are still on, but we can hear with our spiritual ears through the everyday clatter. Two other Scriptures are: Ezekiel 11:19—given a new heart and Psalm

27:14—take courage.

The third line of the song states, "I search forever for You." Searching seems to be something we spend a lot of time doing, such as searching for everyday things we lose or misplace (keys, books, pens, et cetera). Also, we search for peace, contentment, patience, and joy. The first searches are material things. (He can help us find these, too.) The second are more spiritual. We are really searching for Him and want to follow His instructions; for we, as Christ Followers, know that He is our only source of peace, contentment, patience, and joy.

"You search the Scriptures, because you think that in them you have eternal life; and it is these that bear witness to Me," (John 5:39 NAS). His Word, His Scripture, bears Him witness that what He tells us is the truth. Without Christ, we cannot know Him!

Check my heart, God. See if there is any wickedness there. Reveal to me what You know about me! "O Lord, Thou hast searched me and known me. Thou dost know when I sit down and when I rise up; Thou dost understand my thoughts from afar," (Psalm 139:1–2 NAS). God wants us to understand Him more, and then we can be more understanding of others. His Word says, "Searching for it like a prospector panning for gold, like an adventurer on a treasure hunt, believe Me before you know it Fear-of-God will be yours; you'll have come upon the knowledge of God," (Proverbs 24–5, The Message Bible). More Scriptures are: Proverbs 20:27 and Judges 5:16.

We need to give ourselves a mental and spiritual checkup occasionally and not make excuses when we see something we don't like. (See Galatians 6:3–4 and I Corinthians 11:27–30.)

I finished the song with "How merciful You are; Healing in Your hands; We Your children are safe in Your arms." We know of His mercy. "O give thanks unto the Lord; for He is good; for His mercy endureth forever," (1 Chronicles 16:34 KJV). His mercies for us are truly astonishing! Paul quoted God in Romans 9:15: "For He said to Moses, 'I will have mercy on whom I will have mercy....'"

Even when we were "dead" in our trespasses, God had mercy on us by sending His Son as our living sacrifice. "By grace we have been saved," (Ephesians 2:5 NAS). Also read James 5:11.

"Who Himself bore our sins in His own body on the tree, that we, having died to sins, might live for righteousness—by whose stripes you were healed," (1 Peter 2:24 NKJV). Healing comes through Jesus Christ, whether it is miraculous or earthly. He was wounded horribly so that we wouldn't have to go through what He went through. His stripes have healed us from the "infection and death" our sins would have required of us. Aeneas was paralyzed for years; and Peter commanded him, in the name of Jesus Christ to rise and walk, (Acts 9:34). Other Scriptures are James 5:16 and Revelation 22:22—healing of the nations.

Jesus loves the children! He was indignant with His disciples when they tried to keep the children away from Him. "Permit the children to come to Me; do not hinder them; for the kingdom of God belongs to such as these," (Mark 10:14 NAS). The children are so loved because they accept Jesus as He is. They believe in Him without reservations or doubt. He tells them He is their Savior, and they believe Him! It is in the manner of the children, believing and trusting, that Christ wants us to come to Him at all times.

CRUMBS FROM THE MASTER'S TABLE: NOW WE HAVE COME TO THE END OF THIS SONG. I HOPE WE HAVE TRULY DECIDED THERE IS NO ONE LIKE JESUS AND GIVE HIM OUR FOREVER DEVOTION AND LOVE.

Aid And Comfort

SCRIPTURE: PSALM 46:1 (NAS)

*"God is our refuge and strength, a very present
help in trouble."*

We like to sing choruses in our church services, and one of our
favorites tells of God being our refuge. I have sung this song many
times; but as we sang it one night, it took on a new meaning to me.
As I listened to the words, I thought of the Scripture verse in
Psalms.

"God is our refuge and strength." When I think of a refuge, I
think of some place I can go where I can get out of the storm and
rain, some place safe and secure. My home is the refuge I love best
because I feel warm and safe there. But the warmest, most secure
and safe place I want to be, when the storms and rain of this life are
all around me, is in the arms of my loving God. I want those com-
forting, soft, strong arms around me that will never fail. He is my
refuge!

The second part of the verse is, "A very present help in trouble."
God is always here for us, never far away when we need Him.
Friends are wonderful to have, and God-given friends are more

precious than diamonds and rubies. God gives us these friends to be our human contact that we need. But as wonderful as they are, we could lose them. We can never lose God and His "present help" when we are His children. He knows our troubles and the answer to them. All we have to do to keep us in His arms is put our faith and trust in Him. HE will never let go!

A CRUMB FROM HIS TABLE: "...THE ROCK OF MY STRENGTH, MY REFUGE IS IN GOD."

Are You Washed?

SCRIPTURE: REVELATION 7:14B (NAS)

*"…they have washed their robes and made them
white in the blood of the Lamb."*

Have you ever washed a black cloth in red and it came out white? I don't think it's possible to do. But Jesus can take us, who are black in sin, and wash us in His blood, which makes us "whiter than snow."

When we do not give our life to Jesus, that is, accept Him as the one true Son of God, then we are covered in sin; and God can't see us for the blackness in which sin covers us. We are completely separated from God, the Father, which leads to eternal death. God does not want us to be separated from Him because He made us to fellowship with Him. He loves us so much that He sent His only Son, Jesus, to make a way for us to come out of our darkness and into His Light. The only way He could do that was to sacrifice His Son. Jesus was the perfect lamb without a blemish sent to be our atonement. He shed His blood for our sins so that we are washed in His blood and are white in the eyes of God. Now God can see us! We can walk with Him, talk with Him, "eat" with Him, and

13

fellowship in every way with Him. Oh, Glorious God!

A CRUMB FROM HIS TABLE: "WHAT IS MAN, THAT THOU DOST TAKE THOUGHT OF HIM?" (PSALM 8:4F NAS).

Beauty Of Holiness

SCRIPTURE: JOHN 13:9 (NAS)

"Simon Peter said to Him, 'Lord, not my feet only, but also my hands and my head.'"

On Thanksgiving a few years ago, we spent the day with our Aunt Sue, out on her ranch. Her ranch is miles from any town, and you have to get to it through woods and swamps—no paved roads there! It is like going back in time to pioneer Florida, just as God made it—a beautiful, restful place. I feel so close to God out there and exalt in the natural beauty provided by Him.

The next day I was reading in the book of John and was reminded of God's creation. I love the book of John. No wonder he was our Lord's "beloved disciple." In chapter thirteen, we learn the lesson of humility. Lord, how You like to teach us by doing! Imagine our Lord Jesus, the creator of everything, God's own Son and the King of Kings, humbling Himself as a lowly slave or servant and washing the feet of unimportant people (the world would call them). He was teaching His followers that if it was not beneath Him to care for even the one who would betray Him, nothing should be beneath us who love and follow Him. We are to love and help other believers, as well as those who are lost. Lord, teach me to be a servant with a servant's heart, as You are.

CRUMBS FROM HIS TABLE: "THANK YOU, LORD, FOR REMINDING ME WHOSE I AM. I JUST WANT TO SAY THANK YOU AGAIN FOR GIVING ME ANOTHER DAY IN A PLACE IN FLORIDA THAT IS STILL UNTOUCHED BY CIVILIZATION. IN THOSE WOODS AND SWAMPS, I WAS SURROUNDED BY YOUR MAGNIFICENT HAND OF CREATION."

Being Thankful In Our Catastrophe

SCRIPTURE: PSALM 100 (NAS)

"Shout joyfully to the Lord, all the earth. Serve the Lord with gladness; come before His presence with singing. Know that the Lord Himself is God; it is He who has made us, and not we ourselves; we are His people and the sheep of His pasture. Enter His gates with thanksgiving, and His courts with praise. Give thanks to Him, bless His name. For the Lord is good; His loving kindness is everlasting, and His faithfulness to all generations."

Our beautiful church building burned tonight. We had such a meaningful service this morning, and we could feel the Spirit moving over the congregation. Our pastor, Dr. David Myers, preached a sermon on soul winning. Part of his message was on Philip witnessing to the Ethiopian—how the Spirit told Philip to go, and Philip went without hesitation. We are to go, without hesitation, when the Spirit nudges us, even if it is just across the room.

Maybe you wonder why I started this writing with the 100th Psalm. It is because God wants us to be thankful even in our catastrophes. Paul wrote in Ephesians 5:20, "Always give thanks for all things in the name of our Lord Jesus Christ to God, even the Father."

I know this seems impossible at times; but Paul knew that when we are thanking the Lord for "all" things, our minds will be on Him and what He can do for us—not on ourselves and what we can do.

Our church building may be destroyed, but God's church body that met in that building is not destroyed! We know that God can make something wonderful out of our loss. Isn't it going to be a great experience in our faith and trust in Mighty God to see the things He is going to do? The aftermath of the loss of our church building will be an once-in-a-lifetime opportunity to show our city and surrounding area just how much we love and trust Christ as we "joyfully" go about His business of restoring the church building and showing them WE are the church, Northridge, First Baptist Church, Haines City, Florida. The church is not the building. We will never have a better chance of showing the lost people around us how much Jesus means to us.

At times, such as we are going through now, we need more than ever to look to God's Word for comfort, strength and encouragement. Let me quote a few Scriptures that comfort me:

"Fear thou not; for I am with thee; be not dismayed, for I am thy God. I will strengthen thee; yea, I will help thee; yea, I will uphold thee with the right hand of my righteousness," (Isaiah 41:10 ASV).

"But they that wait upon the Lord shall renew their strength; they shall mount up with wings as eagles; they shall run and not be weary; and they shall walk, and not faint," (Isaiah 40:31 KJV).

"Even them will I bring to My Holy mountain and make them joyful in my house of prayer: their burnt offerings and their sacrifices shall be accepted upon mine altar; for mine house shall be called an house of prayer for all people," (Isaiah 56:7 KJV).

CRUMBS FROM HIS TABLE: I KNOW THERE ARE MANY MORE SCRIPTURES THAT WOULD BE RIGHT FOR US AT THIS TIME. "...IF THERE IS ANY EXCELLENCE AND IF ANYTHING WORTHY OF PRAISE, LET YOUR MIND DWELL ON THESE THINGS." (PHILIPPIANS 4:8B NAS).

Bow Of Promise

SCRIPTURE: GENESIS 9:12–15 (NAS)
"I set My bow in the cloud, and it shall be for a sign of a covenant between Me and the earth," (Verse 13).

At times your life may seem to be rough; your role in life may be hard. You may even feel like throwing in the towel. But when you see God's rainbow after a storm, just remember that God is in control. He still watches over His own and abundantly gives you grace, courage, and strength to meet life's challenges.

Noah and his family were saved in the ark from the flood that God sent to destroy the wicked earth. God promised Noah He would never destroy the earth by water again but would destroy it by fire. As Noah escaped the flood, we can escape the fire by being in Christ, Who is the ark of our salvation.

Someday God will shut the door into Christ just as He shut the door into the ark. Then it will be too late for those outside of Christ. Once we are in Christ, we can have the eternal assurance of the rainbow that encircles God's throne.

CRUMBS FROM HIS TABLE: "...THAT WHOEVER BELIEVES MAY IN HIM HAVE ETERNAL LIFE," (JOHN 3:15 NAS).

Do I Really Care?

SCRIPTURE: PSALM 51:10, 13 (NAS)

"Create in me a clean heart, O God, and renew a steadfast spirit within me. Then I will teach transgressors Thy ways, and sinners will be converted to Thee."

Remember the story of Jonah? Jonah ran from God because he did not want to do what God had told him to do. He ran away and hid (he thought) on a ship, but he could not escape God. A great storm came upon the ship, and the sailors tossed Jonah overboard. A great fish swallowed him, and he stayed in the stomach of the fish for three days and nights (as Jesus was in the grave for three days). He prayed to God, and God commanded him to go to Nineveh to tell the people of the doom that awaited them if they did not repent of their sinful ways.

Then Jonah was angry when God did not destroy Nineveh, even though the city had repented. Jonah was really pouting because God had not let the doom fall on Nineveh.

He made a shelter for himself, and God caused a vine to grow on the shelter to provide shade for his head. Jonah was extremely happy about the plant. Then God caused the plant to wither and die which angered Jonah, so he told God he wanted to die.

God accused Jonah of loving and grieving over the vine and not grieving over the lost people in Nineveh. God asked Jonah if He should have more compassion for the plant than the city of 120,000 people.

God was asking Jonah if he really cared.

God could and is asking the same question to us today. Do I really care about the lost people of my city, or do I worry about the "plants" of my life?

What are the "plants" of my life? What do I do, Lord, that is more important than telling a lost friend or family member about You? How many people has the Holy Spirit brought to my mind for me to give them the good news of my Savior? I know I am a guilty one.

When I say I am concerned over the ones who are lost, do I really care? Or am I like Jonah, trying to hide or run away from God? Jonah found that a ship, a storm, and even a big fish could not hide him from God.

How much better our lives would be if we stopped trying to hide behind excuses and our "good works" from God, who always knows where we are and what is in our hearts.

God says that I don't have to save the lost. That's His job. I only have to tell them about His Son, what He has done for them, and that He loves them.

CRUMBS FROM HIS TABLE: LORD, I'M GLAD IT'S NOT UP TO ME TO "SAVE" ANYONE. MY JOB IS TO TELL THEM ABOUT YOU.

Don't Leave The Lord Jesus At Church

SCRIPTURE: JOSHUA 24:15 (NAS)

"...but as for me and my house, we will serve the Lord."

When you go to the church house, do you expect to encounter Jesus, or do you simply go out of duty? If you do encounter Him, is it an unexpected bonus?

When you meet Jesus in your church, don't leave Him there when you go home. Jesus wants to be important to you at home as well as at church. He is not just a Sunday morning Lord. We are to make Him Lord of our homes, as well as Lord of our lives. So when you leave church from now on, don't leave Jesus there. Take Him home with you.

Joshua said to his people in Joshua 24:15, "As for me and my house, we will serve the Lord." Joshua didn't say, "As for me and my church, we will serve the Lord." He said his house or home.

When we take Jesus home with us, we WILL serve Him! We don't want to do anything else.

A CRUMB FROM HIS TABLE: YOUR HOME WILL BE THE HAPPIEST PLACE

23

IN THE WORLD WHEN YOU TAKE JESUS HOME WITH YOU AND MAKE HIM LORD.

Don't Let The Door Shut You Out!

SCRIPTURE: GENESIS 7:1, 7, 12, 21 (KJV)

"Then the Lord said to Noah, 'Come thou and all thy house into the ark; for thee have I seen righteous before Me in this generation.' And Noah went in, and his wife, and his sons' wives with them because of the water of the flood. And the rain was on the earth for forty days and forty nights. And all flesh died that moved upon the earth."

The story in Genesis about the flood and God saving Noah and his family is a familiar one. Sometimes the problem with the familiarity of the best-known Bible stories is we tend to read them and not "listen" to the message God has for us.

In the story of the ark, we know God only allowed eight people to be saved among the thousands who lived on earth during Noah's lifetime. I thank God I am living on this side of the flood and not on the other side. I wonder if I would have believed Noah when he preached the coming end of creation. I could have been one of those who must have banged on the ark's door and screamed, "Let me in!"

Being on "this side" of the cross of Christ means that I can look back at Noah and know what Noah knew, which the lost didn't.

When God closed the door to the ark, the people, who were left outside, were doomed. This same thing is true today. When God closes the "door" to salvation, unsaved people are doomed. We know God sends His Holy Spirit to deal with the lost ones' hearts but will not always strive with them, (Psalm 103:9 and Genesis 6:3). "NOW IS THE DAY OF SALVATION," Paul has told us in 2 Corinthians 6:2. My prayer is that all have an intimate, personal relationship with our Lord Jesus; and if not, please, don't wait until the door is closed.

There is another door that is opened to us as Christ Followers. This door leads into the "room of the knowledge of God." God is standing at the door, inviting us in. Where is this door? It is the front cover of our Bibles. Open it prayerfully and give it the full attention it deserves. Let the Holy Spirit of God lead you into the treasure of words He has especially for you. He will reveal the knowledge of Himself that you need to know at the time. "The fear of the Lord is the beginning of wisdom; a good understanding have all those who do HIS commandments. His praise endures forever," (Psalm 111:10 NAS). "The fear of the Lord is the beginning of knowledge," (Proverbs 1:7 NAS).

In our search for knowledge of God, we must ask, "What do You want me to know, Lord?" Then we must listen and watch for His answers. Take time to wait for His revelation of the Word, (Acts 15:17–18 and Isaiah 48:3).

God wants us to learn His knowledge by reading, listening to Him, and by listening and reading words from His anointed messengers. Not all preachers and lay preachers are His messengers. We must pray and ask God for wisdom to know the difference.

Why does God care whether we have His knowledge or not? Because the more we know about Him (His character, love, and wisdom), the more we love and understand Him. We will never completely understand God, but we can know more about Him and His ways than we know today. The more we know Him, the more we want to know which results in a closer relationship with Him.

Don't put off getting to know more about God. NOW is the

time to start reading and listening to Him. The longer we wait to communicate with Him, the more of His wisdom and revelation we miss. Think of reading His Word as an exciting book (which it is). Hang on to the last word you read and be anxious to read what He has in store for you next!

God will close the door to His "room of knowledge," as He closed the door to the ark. "For this reason, we must pay much closer attention to what we have heard lest we drift away from it," (Hebrews 2:1 NAS). If we neglect the word and the knowledge of God, we are in danger of losing our first joy. We will not lose our salvation, but we will remain only "drinking the milk" of the Word and not joining Him in the great banquet which He has planned for us. "Therefore, leaving the elementary teaching about the Christ, let us press on to maturity," (Hebrews 6:1 NAS).

God will abundantly bless us as we seek Him and more knowledge of Him.

CRUMBS FROM HIS TABLE: "HAPPY IS THE MAN THAT FINDETH WISDOM, AND THE MAN THAT GETTETH UNDERSTANDING. FOR THE MERCHANDISE OF IT IS BETTER THAN THE MERCHANDISE OF SILVER, AND THE GAIN THEREOF THAN FINE GOLD," (PROVERBS 3: 13–14 KJV).

Faith For Today

SCRIPTURE: HEBREWS 11:1 (NAS)
*"Now faith is the assurance of things hoped for,
the conviction of things not seen."*

I think of faith as something that is just a common belief I have in Jesus as Lord. I know I can't claim Him as my Savior without faith in Him. I have always taken faith for granted. But, today, the Holy Spirit had me focus on faith. Not just the word, but I began thinking about the meaning of faith.

I always thought faith was what God had given me to believe in Him and His Son. I thought that my faith was for now and into the future. But He told me, "Not so."

The faith He gives to me today will be sufficient for me today. It is not the same amount or quality that I needed yesterday. God didn't promise us a future of tomorrows; He only promised us one day at a time. Therefore, He knows if we will have a tomorrow, what our needs will be, and what faith we will need to take care of another day. He tells us in His Word, "Therefore, do not be anxious for tomorrow; for tomorrow will care for itself," (Matthew 6:30 NAS).

29

When our tomorrows, which God gives us, come, He will give us the faith we need to deal with life's problems and joys for that day.

Does God do this for everyone? No. We must believe and accept His Son, Jesus, as our Lord and Savior. This takes faith to believe; we also must walk with His Son day after day, loving and staying in communication with Him constantly! "So faith comes from hearing, and hearing by the Word of Christ," (Romans 10:17 NAS). This is the way our faith increases in Him, and He increases His faith in us. We won't know how great a faith we have until we meet Jesus face to face.

A CRUMB FROM HIS TABLE: "AND WITHOUT FAITH IT IS IMPOSSIBLE TO PLEASE HIM...." (HEBREWS 11:6 NAS).

Feathers Of Blessings

SCRIPTURE: PSALM 91:4 (KJV)

"He shall cover thee with His feathers, and under His wings shalt thou trust."

My husband, Bill, and I sit on our back porch nearly every morning, drinking our cups of coffee. We love to watch the squirrels, doves, and other birds as they come for their morning meal. Bill feeds them all, so we have a mini-animal sanctuary in our back yard. We even have three tiny mice living in one of our drain pipes!

As I was sitting on our porch one morning, I watched some doves in the yard eating bread that had been scattered about. Suddenly, something frightened them, causing them to swiftly fly away. In their flight, they sent a shower of feathers raining slowly to the ground.

The feathers, as they softly fell, reminded me of the great blessings that come to us from God above. God doesn't send torrents of blessings; they fall gently on our spirits, like the gently falling feathers.

God knows that we wouldn't be able to handle all of His blessings at once, so He gives them to us one at a time. He has given so many blessings to me in my lifetime that I now have a downpour.

God's blessings, unlike raindrops, do not disappear into the ground. Once He gives them to us, they are ours to keep forever!

The newest blessing God is giving to me is helping me see Him in everything, such as the blessing of seeing Him in the falling feathers.

Thank you, Lord God, for this major blessing.

A CRUMB FROM HIS TABLE: SHOWERS OF BLESSINGS FROM GOD ARE WHAT WE PLEAD FOR.

Feed The Flock

SCRIPTURE: JOHN 21:15–17 (KJV)

"He said to him the third time, 'Simon, son of Jonas, loveth thou Me,'" (Verse 17).

It's interesting that Jesus asked Simon Peter three times if he loved Him. This is the same number of times that Peter had denied Christ. I'm sure Peter, after denying Christ, felt as if he were outside of the disciple group who had followed Jesus for three years. Jesus is now questioning him, "Do you love Me?" Certainly, after the third time Jesus asked this, Peter was deeply hurt.

Perhaps Peter was remembering the times he had denied Jesus and thought Jesus didn't believe him. But Jesus knows everything! He knew what was hurting Peter: he was afraid of being rejected by Jesus.

In commanding Peter to "feed My lambs, shepherd My sheep, tend My sheep," Jesus was getting Peter to affirm his love for Him and showing Peter that He wanted him in the ministry. Jesus, the good Shepherd, has finally turned Peter, the fisherman, into a shepherd himself. Peter had been completely restored and followed Jesus passionately for the rest of his life.

Is Jesus asking me today, "Do you love Me?" I need to search my heart everyday to see if there is anything my Lord might see in me that He would ask me that question. Am I feeding His sheep? Am I aware that His sheep need to be fed? His command is "Feed My sheep," not just once but every day that He gives me. My prayer today is, "Lord, give me the spiritual food to feed Your lambs."

CRUMBS FROM HIS TABLE: "HE SAID TO HIM, 'TEND MY LAMBS.'"

From Riches To Rags

SCRIPTURE: LUKE 2:1–20 (NAS)
*"And she gave birth to her first-born son; and she wrapped
Him in cloths and laid Him in a manger, because there was no
room for them in the inn," (Verse 7).*

How many times I have read this verse in Luke, I cannot count. But
as I searched the Gospels to read again the account of Jesus' birth,
I found only Matthew and Luke actually gave a description of His
birth. After reading Luke's story, I began to really read again and
listen to the words of this familiar story, as if for the first time.

Verse seven especially caught my attention. Mary, being heavy
with her child, began the pain of birth that would bring forth the
newborn Son. Imagine her, the one chosen by God to be the mother
of His Son, the Prince of heaven, giving birth to Him in a stable—
not a big, beautiful, kingly palace, but a place that was made to
shelter animals.

This, of course, was typical of Jesus, who once said, "…the Son
of Man has nowhere to lay His head," (Matthew 8:20 NAS). We
learn that all of His life in ministry was spent walking about the
country with His disciples, teaching and healing people. He had
crowds of people around Him most of the time; however, His was

35

a lonely life, because of His great task ahead of Him. He was God's perfect solution to sinful people: Jesus' death, burial, and resurrection.

At Christmas we celebrate His birthday by giving gifts to one another. But God's gift to us, Jesus Christ, can never be duplicated or topped. It is eternal life with Him for eternity.

CRUMBS FROM HIS TABLE: WITHOUT HIS BIRTH, THERE COULD NOT HAVE BEEN HIS DEATH AND RESURRECTION.

God Heals

SCRIPTURE: 2 CHRONICLES 7:14 (NAS)

"...and my people who are called by My name humble themselves and pray, and seek My face and turn from their wicked ways, then I will hear from heaven, will forgive their sin, and will heal their land."

In the dedication of the temple which Solomon had built, God's glory was very evident: "And the priests could not enter into the house of the LORD, because the glory of the LORD filled the LORD's house," (2 Chronicles 7:2 NAS). This great glory of God's is called the "Shekinah Glory," which means "a word expressing the glory and presence of God." Verse three tells of the sons of Israel seeing the fire and the glory of God coming down on the house. God allowed the Israelites to see His glory and fire because they had been obedient to Him.

That reminds me of a Sunday a few years ago when we experienced the "Shekinah Glory" come down in our church. It was during the morning worship service that people suddenly started going down to the front of the sanctuary, and the steps in front of the pulpit became an altar. Many began going forward to the pastor, asking for prayer for salvation and healing, as they cried and praised the Lord. More and more people continued going forward, singing and praising the Lord. Since then, our church has not been the same. We changed from a typical church to a Holy Spirit filled one and started reaching people for Christ. We are still this church today and even more so.

God not only sent His glory to the people of Israel, but He promised to send locusts or pestilence to them if they ceased to obey and worship Him, (2 Chronicles 7:13). However, He also promised to hear their prayers asking for forgiveness and to heal their land.

God's promises still apply to us today. We may not have "locusts and pestilence," but we have destructive ways that mean eternal death for us. So many evils of this day could be called "locusts and pestilence," such as abortion, adultery, drugs, lies, and anything ungodly. God could have already destroyed us if it weren't for the Christ Followers who have (and are) praying for this nation. God has promised that if we "turn from our wicked ways," He will "hear our prayers and heal our land."

A CRUMB FROM HIS TABLE: "...FOR THE LORD YOUR GOD IS HE WHO FIGHTS FOR YOU, JUST AS HE PROMISED YOU."

God Sings!

SCRIPTURE: ZEPHANIAH 3:17 (KJV)

"The Lord thy God in the midst of thee is mighty; He will save, He well rejoice over thee with joy; He will rest in His love, He will joy over thee with singing."

Dear Lord, I love You today more than I did yesterday because You've given me one more day for my love to grow.

I heard a Scripture read on the radio as I was making up my bed. (By the way, Lord, thank You for my bed.) The Scripture is the one written above. I am so excited over this verse! To think that Almighty God sings over me is almost more than I can comprehend. What have I done, Lord, to be that important to You and loved by You? This beautiful truth has brought tears of joy to my eyes. You have set my heart to singing, Lord, and I hope I am harmonizing with You! I will remember to "joy" over people.

Lord God, You are my salvation, my joy, my love of heart and soul, my best friend, my counselor, my judge, my creator, and my soon-coming King.

Thank You, Lord, for giving me special Scriptures to read and "hide" in my heart. I ask You, Lord, to let me be able to share this beautiful promise with others.

CRUMBS FROM HIS TABLE: DEAR LORD, JUST THE SOUND OF YOUR NAME, "JESUS," SENDS MY SPIRIT SINGING AND PRAISING YOU.

God's Eternal Power

SCRIPTURE: SONG OF SOLOMON 2:1 (NAS)
"I AM the rose of Sharon, the lily of the valleys."

We can see God's eternal power in many things in His natural world. The rose is one thing in which we can see God and His eternal way. We see the beautiful bloom of the rose, but it will soon wither and die; however, the rose bush itself is still alive. Eventually, the bush will need to be pruned. As long as the bush's roots are in the good earth, it is alive. Then, soon it will sprout out leaves and branches and bloom again.

We are like the rose bush. The earth is God, and as long as our "roots" are in Him, we are alive and produce "blooms" (works) for Him.

When sin comes into our lives, God "prunes" our sins from us after we ask Him for forgiveness.

This rose bush and we can be eternal and natural as long as we are in God and His "good earth" (His will).

A CRUMB FROM HIS TABLE: HE IS THE LILY OF THE VALLEY, AS THE

VERSE SAYS. IN HIM ALONE I LIVE AND HAVE ALL I NEED TO CLEANSE AND MAKE ME WHOLE IN HIS SIGHT.

God's Mission For Us

SCRIPTURE: JOHN 6:47 (NAS)
"Truly, truly, I say to you, he who believes has eternal life."

God knows who will accept Jesus as their Lord and be saved. John 6:44 says, "No one can come to Me (Jesus) unless the Father (God) who sent me, draws him." I think this is FATHER, the HOLY SPIRIT, who draws people to Jesus.

Why, then, does God want us to go and tell everyone about Jesus and that He died and rose again to save us from our sin? One reason is because we don't know who will believe and who will not. Therefore, we must tell ALL people about Jesus. Another reason may be God is giving them one more chance to be saved. He also wants to know who obeys His command to "Go therefore and make disciples of all the nations, baptizing them in the name of the Father and the Son and the Holy Spirit," (Matthew 28:19 NAS).

CRUMBS FROM HIS TABLE: "GOD, I'M READY TO GO WHERE YOU WANT ME TO GO—EVEN IF IT MEANS STAYING WHERE I AM."

He Rolled Away
The Stone

SCRIPTURE: LUKE 24:1–2 (KJV)

"…very early in the morning, they came unto the sepulcher…; And they found the stone rolled away…."

I was wandering through this worldly garden, and all the weeds of sin were dragging me down as darkness was all around me. I was lost in this garden of everyday problems, burdens, and temptations. All seemed to be hopeless, which resulted in feelings of being lost, alone, and desperate. I thought, "O Lord, where are You?" It was more of a thought than a plea.

But, what is it that I see? It seems to be a faint light. There is a light ahead that seems to get brighter as I go toward it. Though my heart is heavy as if a stone is in it, it seems to get lighter as I go toward the glow.

Suddenly, I see a most GLORIOUS LIGHT! There He is! It's got to be JESUS! This "Light of the World" has guided me to Him!

I see the empty tomb. There by the entrance is the "big" stone that was the burden in my heart.

JESUS rolled the stone away. Now I am free and will have the

JOY OF JESUS in my heart forever.

I never have to carry heavy burdens again. I can give them all to Jesus, and He will always roll them away!

A CRUMB FROM HIS TABLE: "…GOD IS LIGHT, AND IN HIM THERE IS NO DARKNESS AT ALL." 1 JOHN 1:5 (KJV)

Hear And Do

SCRIPTURE: JAMES 1:22–25 (KJV)
"But be ye doers of the Word, and not hearers only."

As I was reading the book of James, I was especially drawn to the verses in chapter one. That book is one of my favorites in the Bible because it is "meat" and not "milk" to Christ Followers. James (the brother of Jesus) can get my attention. He teaches faith, perseverance, wisdom, and many other things I need to hear and heed.

As I was reading James 1:22–25, the Spirit held my attention there. I know when He does this, He has something for me. I read and re-read prayerfully, waiting for His insight into these words.

James says for us to be doers, not just hearers; for if we are merely hearers, we are just looking and moving on. If we simply hear the words of Jesus and not act on them, we are missing the blessings and knowledge He has to give us. We will remember things we do and tend to forget things we hear and read.

I think this is one reason Jesus wants us to be servants. So we can experience the blessings and pleasures that come from doing and not just hearing.

When we look at His commandments and do His commands, we are set free in our spirits and will to become better servants than we have ever been. James tells us we will be effectual in what we do in the name of Jesus, and be blessed in what we do.

CRUMBS FROM HIS TABLE: LORD, BLESS ALL OF THE DOERS OF YOUR WORDS AND HELP ALL OF THE HEARERS TO LOOK INTENTLY TO YOU FOR DIRECTIONS ON BECOMING YOUR SERVANTS.

His Own

SCRIPTURE: DEUTERONOMY 7:6 (KJV)

"For you art an holy people unto the Lord thy God: the Lord thy God hath chosen thee to be a special people unto Himself, above all the people that are upon the face of the earth."

What a wonderful verse in Scripture to encourage us to persevere for our Lord God. Moses is speaking what may have been his farewell address to the Israelites. This verse is meant for us today as it was meant for them thousands of years ago.

Moses is telling us we are special to our Lord God because He has chosen us to be His holy people. We have been chosen from all of the millions of people on earth. For what has God chosen us? That is what the Pharisees thought, and they lost God. If we act this way, is our salvation real?

We have a great responsibility as God's chosen people. We are to love Him as He loves us; we are to continuously be thankful for the gift of salvation through His Son, Jesus Christ. We are to persevere diligently to keep believing in Him and telling others about Him; we are to never lose hope in our Lord but always remember whose we are and love Him as He loves us, unconditionally.

A CRUMB FROM HIS TABLE: LORD, HELP ME TO LOVE YOU MORE TODAY THAN I DID YESTERDAY BUT NOT AS MUCH AS I WILL TOMORROW.

I Did It

SCRIPTURE: JOHN 19:1–2, 6, 18, 34 (NAS)
"Then Pilate therefore took Jesus, and scourged Him. And the soldiers wove a crown of thorns and put it on His head, and arrayed Him in a purple robe… When therefore the chief priests and the officers saw Him, they cried out saying, 'Crucify, crucify!' Pilate said to them, 'Take Him yourselves, and crucify Him, for I find no guilt in Him.' There they crucified Him, and with Him two other men, one on either side, and Jesus in between. …but one of the soldiers pierced His side with a spear, and immediately there came out blood and water."

SCRIPTURE: MARK 15:19–20 (NAS)
"And they kept beating His head with a reed, and spitting at Him, and kneeling and bowing before Him. And after they had mocked Him, they took the purple off Him, and put His garments on Him. And they led Him out to crucify Him."

I have taught an adult ladies' Sunday School class for many years. On one Sunday morning, as I was bringing to a close our lesson for that day, something was said about Jesus' crucifixion. Suddenly, these thoughts came pouring into my mind:

Jesus was scourged: the Roman soldiers didn't scourge Him—I did.

The soldiers didn't weave a crown of thorns for His head—I did.

The soldiers didn't give Him blows to His face—I did.

The priests and people didn't call out, "Crucify Him!"—I did.

51

The soldiers didn't beat His head with a reed—I did.
They didn't spit on Him—I did.
They didn't mock Him—I did.
The Roman soldiers didn't nail Him to the cross—I did.
The soldier didn't pierce His side with a spear—I did!

When I have spoken His name other than in reverence, I scourged Him. I wove that crown of thorns when I depended on self rather than Him. I gave Him blows when I took credit for something He had done. I cried, "Crucify Him," when I did not stand up for HIM as my Lord and Savior. Beating His head and spitting on Him and mocking Him happens every time I draw away from Him. It was me and all my SIN that nailed Him to that horrible cross. I pierced His side every time I have doubted Him. How could He love me as much as He does and give me the precious gift of eternal life with Him, after all I have done to Him?

A CRUMB FROM HIS TABLE: JESUS SAID, "I LOVE YOU THIS MUCH," AS HE SPREAD OUT HIS ARMS ON THE CROSS AND DIED.

I Trust You, Father

SCRIPTURE: ISAIAH 51:7–8; LUKE 10:17–20;
22:31–32; AND PSALM 91:11 (NAS):

*"For He will give His angels charge concerning you,
to guard you in all your ways."*

Some of the marvelous promises and blessings we get from our Father God are listed in the Scriptures above. The only way we can receive these blessings is to accept and know His Son Jesus as our Lord and Savior. Then we can have all of the gifts God has reserved for us. But we must have a close relationship with Him and study His word so we know for what to ask Him.

I have found in my life when I am hurt by someone I love, I must go to my Father God for consolation and help. All I have to do is open my Bible, and He will guide me to the Scripture He knows I need. But this Scripture He gives me is not going to do me any good if I don't read it and listen to hear the comfort it gives me.

When friends you love hurt you, it's like hurting a part of your body. However, when family hurts you, it's a great pain and ache in your heart. This heart-pain lasts and hurts much longer.

When this happens to me, I run to my heavenly Father just like

I used to run to my Daddy when I was a child and was hurt.

How thankful I am for my Heavenly Father and His Son, Jesus, and for His Holy Spirit! I don't have just one to comfort me; I have all three! The Scriptures above show me just how much I am loved.

A CRUMB FROM HIS TABLE: I WILL SAY TO THE LORD, "MY REFUGE AND MY FORTRESS, MY GOD IN WHOM I TRUST," (PSALM 91:2 NAS).

I've Just Seen Jesus

SCRIPTURE: PSALM 66:5 (NAS)
"Come and see the works of God, Who is awesome in His deeds toward the sons of men."

We have a small cabin in the mountains of North Georgia, where I can see the handwork of God everywhere I look. Sitting on the porch of the cabin, I can look at the trees that surround me. No matter if it is spring, summer, fall, or winter, the trees are always beautiful. I can see Jesus.

In the spring, the trees are putting on their "Easter" clothes of bright green leaves, decorated with the flowers of mountain laurel and rhododendron. The summer trees are a darker green with thicker vegetation. In fall, the trees are indescribably beautiful with the gold, yellow, brown, orange, and green leaves decorating their limbs. There is an ethereal beauty about the winter trees with their stark, bare branches awaiting the time God replaces their leaves. I can see Jesus.

I see Jesus in the creek, whose water rushes from an unknown source to join the river, which is not far away.

I see Jesus in the faces of the people in the First Baptist Church of Helen, who enthusiastically greet me when I enter into the building.

As we ride around the area at dusk looking for deer, we are as excited as children when we spot one. They stand so still; they are like statues—such beautiful creatures only God could create. I can see Jesus.

On our way back home to Haines City, Florida, the changes in the day are spectacular! The early morning brings the beautiful sunrise that spills out over the land. Then, here comes the bright sun and the beginnings of a cloudy sky on the horizon. Eventually we meet the rain, and it comes and cleanses the roads we travel, as well as our car.

Then, as the sky clears, we see God's handwork in the white fluffy clouds that seem to mock the rain clouds, saying, "You can't keep us away!"

As the sun sets, our Father paints the evening sky in baby blue, fading into baby pink. A child once commented on the amazingly beautiful sunset, "Such lovely!"

CRUMBS FROM HIS TABLE: WE CAN SEE JESUS IN EVERYTHING HE HAS CREATED. IT IS NOT DIFFICULT TO SEE; JUST PUT ON YOUR "JESUS EYES."

John 17:
The Real Lord's Prayer

SCRIPTURE: JOHN 17:1 (NAS)

"...Father, the hour has come; glorify thy Son..."

The verses in Matthew 6:9–13 and Luke 11:2–4 are called "The Lord's Prayer." Actually, Jesus gave this prayer to His disciples when they asked Him to "teach us to pray." This prayer has been used in churches for many years and is still used today. It has become almost a ritual and has been repeated so much, that it has lost its meaning to many.

It is a model prayer Jesus gave to us to use as our pattern when we pray. It is a way for us to know how and in what order we are to pray: First is adoration to our Father in heaven; second is intercession for others; third is petition to God for our daily needs; fourth is repentance for our sins; and the fifth is deliverance (save us from ourselves).

The real Lord's Prayer is John seventeen. It is also called "The High Priestly Prayer."

In this prayer, Jesus is "lifting up His eyes to heaven," talking to His Heavenly Father as only the Son can. He knows it is time for

Him to complete His appointed mission on this earth, and He is asking that He only glorify the Father. God has given Him "authority over all mankind" and many followers. To those who follow Jesus, the Heavenly Father has given eternal life with Him. Life forever with Him means they will know the Father as the "only true God" and know Jesus as Lord.

Jesus says He has glorified God the Father on this earth and has accomplished the task His Father had given Him.

The Lord in these verses (five through eight) is asking His Father to glorify Him with the glory He had when He created the earth.

He became God in the flesh; and as His ministry began, He gathered men, whom God had given Him, out of this world. They were true men of God and kept God's word.

Jesus is still gathering men and women to Himself out of this world. The instructions and ministry Jesus gave to His early disciples, He gives to us today. Nothing has changed in His and God's plan for His true followers except for the years that have passed. We believe in the Word of God and the instructions and blessings that come to us, just as the early men and women believed.

Have you ever thought of Jesus asking Father God for you to become His? In John 17:9, Jesus says, "I ask on their behalf; I do not ask on behalf of the world, but of those whom Thou hast given Me; for they are Thine." I find it overwhelming that Jesus asked God for me! "What is man, that Thou rememberest him..." (Hebrews 2:6 NAS). We who belong to God also belong to Christ—"And all things that are Mine are Thine, and Thine are Mine..." (John 17:10).

Christ has asked His Father to look after us who are still on this earth and prays that His joy be made full in us. Because we are His, we can expect the world to hate us just as it hated Him. Jesus has sanctified us (set us apart) because we are His. We are not of the world, just as He was not of the world.

As God sent His Son into the world, He also sends us into the world. Jesus wants us to be one with Him just as He is one with the Father.

Christ has asked the Father that we who are with the Father be with Jesus so that we may behold His glory. God has loved Jesus from before the foundation of the world, and He is praying for us to share in the great love of God, the Almighty.

It is interesting to note that much of Jesus' priestly prayer is for His followers, then and now. Christ's prayers are never old or obsolete. They are as relevant today as in the time He walked the earth and prayed them.

CRUMBS FROM HIS TABLE: THANK YOU, LORD JESUS, FOR THE PRAYERS YOU PRAYED FOR ME BEFORE I WAS CREATED, AND FOR THE PRAYERS YOU PRAY FOR ME TODAY. HOW WONDERFUL TO KNOW YOU INTERCEDE FOR US BEFORE OUR HEAVENLY FATHER.

"Joint Heirs"

SCRIPTURE: GENESIS 15:5 (KJV)

"And He brought him forth abroad, and said, 'Look now toward heaven, and tell the stars, if thou be able to number them,' and He said unto him, 'So shall thy seed be.'"

God chose Abram (who would become Abraham) to be the father of His nation. The people in this nation were to be God's chosen ones. He would create this great nation of people to be His loyal followers and servants. God told Abraham that he would have as many descendants as there were stars in the heavens. However, God made Abraham wait until he and his wife, Sarah, were very old. God's timing is not the same as ours, (2 Peter 3:8).

God's promise to Abraham was that He would give him a son and would make him (Abraham) the father of a great nation of people. We know God kept His promise. The nation of Israel was numbered in the millions.

I believe God was not only talking about His earthly kingdom but His heavenly kingdom as well. "In hope against hope he believed, in order that he might become a father of many nations, according to that which had been spoken, 'So shall your descendants be,'" (Romans 4:18 NAS).

Through Abraham and his son, Isaac, would come Jesus Christ, the only Son of God. Because Jesus died on the cross so our sins could be forgiven, He makes us children of God when we believe on Him. We are therefore accepted into God's kingdom as His children, and we become part of His heavenly kingdom.

A CRUMB FROM HIS TABLE: "BUT THEY THAT WAIT UPON THE LORD SHALL RENEW THEIR STRENGTH; THEY SHALL MOUNT UP WITH WINGS AS EAGLES; THEY SHALL RUN, AND NOT GET WEARY; AND THEY SHALL WALK, AND NOT FAINT," (ISAIAH 40:31 KJB).

Keep Your Eyes
On The Prize

SCRIPTURE: MATTHEW 14:29–31 (NAS)

"And He (Jesus) said, 'Come!' And Peter got out of the boat, and walked on the water and came toward Jesus. But seeing the wind, he became afraid, and beginning to sink, he cried out, saying, 'Lord, save me!' And immediately Jesus stretched out His hand and took hold of him, and said to him, 'O you of little faith, why did you doubt?'"

Jesus had just fed 5,000 men plus the women and children, (Matthew 14:19–21). Then He made His disciples get into the boat and go ahead of Him to an isolated place to get away from the crowds.

Why did He separate Himself from His followers? He had just finished a successful evangelism service and needed to be alone with His Father because He needed and wanted fellowship and instructions from God.

Lord Jesus, I need You to give me my instructions for today. I have been reading these verses this morning and didn't know why You wanted me to read this Scripture. However, I think I'm beginning to see and am applying it to myself this day.

As I began writing, my husband Bill came in, so I stopped for a few minutes. He began talking about the music in our church services (always a bone of contention among senior adults). We think there are too many new choruses and not enough old hymns. Bill as well as others in our Sunday School class, is struggling with this perceived problem. I, personally, don't care for some of the choruses, but as I have looked around at the congregation, I have seen so many younger people who do like them. So again the Spirit reminds me, "It's not about you, Cherrie—it's all about Jesus."

Verses twenty-five and twenty-six tell about Jesus walking on water to come to the boat where His disciples are. When they saw Him coming, they were frightened and thought He was a ghost. I wonder how many times Jesus walks towards me and I don't recognize Him because I have allowed prejudices to come between us, instead of faith.

"Take courage, it is I," He said. Lord, are you saying it is all right with You for us to sing the choruses? Do they mean as much to You as the old hymns? "Do not be afraid," You said. Are You saying that as long as our praises and thoughts are on You as we sing, You accept it all as praises to You and Your Holiness? As human beings, even when we are saved, we can sing the old hymns without any praises in our heart for You.

Peter tried walking on the water but failed because he took his eyes off of Jesus and saw the wind. Is this what we do? If we are fussing about the choruses versus the old hymns, aren't we taking our eyes off of You and giving something else our full attention? No wonder we have a hard time hearing and seeing You. We let little petty things interrupt our gaze on You. Then we wonder why we have so many tough experiences.

"O you of little faith, why did you doubt?" Our lives are full of doubt when we take our eyes off of Him. The "winds" of doubt that blow us this way and that can be stilled by that quiet voice of our Lord's. When those doubts and negative thoughts come to our minds, they can be eliminated by just saying the precious name of our Savior: "Jesus, Jesus, Jesus."

CRUMBS FROM HIS TABLE: WE MUST LEARN TO RECOGNIZE HIM IN ALL THINGS, EVEN IN CHORUSES AND OLD HYMNS.

Know His Voice

SCRIPTURE: JOHN 10:24–25, 30 (NAS)

"The Jews therefore gathered around Him, and were saying to Him, 'How long will You keep us in suspense? If You are the Christ, tell us plainly.' Jesus answered them, 'I told you, and you do not believe; the works that I do in My Father's name, these bear witness of Me. I and the Father are one.'"

How many times did Jesus try to tell me who He is and what He is before I finally knew? Oh, I knew He was the Son of God, sent to die on the cross for my Sin. I knew this through the Holy Spirit's teaching and revealing His knowledge to me.

The day Jesus revealed to me what I needed and had to have, I fell on my knees and begged Him for it! In John 14:26, Jesus promised, "But the Helper, the Holy Spirit, whom the Father will send in My name, He will teach you all things, and bring to your remembrance all that I said to you." I was determined to stay on my knees until He filled me with the Holy Spirit and made a new person of me. And He did it! Praise the Lord!

He says in John 10:27, "My sheep hear My voice, and I know them, and they follow Me." I could not hear His voice or recognize it before. If I didn't hear His voice and know it, how could I follow Him? There is where my ignorance lay.

Now, I know that sweet, small voice who speaks to me. He speaks in many ways: Sometimes He speaks to me privately, sometimes through a song, sometimes through reading Scriptures, and sometimes in the worship and preaching service. But I know when He is speaking to me. If ever I am out of contact with Him, I know it is my fault and not His. He is always ready to communicate with me.

He also promises in this Scripture that no one shall ever snatch me out of His hand. I know I am safe and with Him forever because He says I am also in the Father's hand, and "He and the Father are one," (John 10:30 NAS).

CRUMBS FROM HIS TABLE: ONE OF SATAN'S GREATEST PLANS IS TO KEEP BELIEVERS UNAWARE OF THE POWER OF THE HOLY SPIRIT IN SPIRIT-FILLED BELIEVERS.

Let's Go Fishing

SCRIPTURE: JOHN 21:6 (NAS)

"And He (Jesus) said to them, 'Cast the net on the right-hand side of the boat, and you will find a catch.'"

Have you caught any fish lately? If not, why? Didn't Jesus tell Peter and Andrew in Matthew 4:19 that He would make them "fishers of men?" Jesus told them this because they were His followers. Have you committed your life to Christ? Are you a follower of His?

Jesus asked His disciples, "'Children, you do not have any fish, do you?' They answered Him, 'No.' And He said to them, 'Cast the net on the right-hand side of the boat, and you will find a catch,'" (John 21:5–6 NAS).

Sometime we are like Peter and Andrew. We fish on the wrong side of the boat without bait. The wrong side of the boat can be when we don't wait on the Holy Spirit to direct us to the one He has prepared to hear and accept the gospel. Are we trying to tell someone about Jesus without praying diligently for that person? If so, we won't have any "bait."

The Holy Spirit is ready to tell you where, when, and how to fish for the best results. If we obey Jesus in fishing on the "right" side of the boat, He promises to give us a "catch" we won't be able to haul in, but HE can!

If you haven't really committed your life to Christ and are not "fishing" where He tells you, pray about doing it today.

A CRUMB FROM HIS TABLE: "AND HE SAID TO THEM, 'FOLLOW ME, AND I WILL MAKE YOU FISHERS OF MEN,'" (MATTHEW 4:19 NAS).

Light In The Forest

SCRIPTURE: ACTS 4:12 (NAS)

*"And there is salvation in no one else; for there is no
other name under heaven that has been given among men,
by which we must be saved."*

As the sun goes down here in the mountains of North Georgia, it
sends rays through the trees and touches a bush like a spotlight. One
bush especially stands out from the darkening trees as if it were a
figure on a stage.

In this way, we as Christ Followers must be. We live in a forest
of people all around us, and we could blend in. Then, no one would
be able to tell us from the "trees."

We cannot and must not let this happen. How can others who
are lost find their way through the "forest" if they have no light to
guide them?

Jesus said, "You are the light of the world…" (Matthew 5:14
NAS). "Let your light shine before men in such a way that they may
see your good works and glorify your Father who is in heaven,"
(Matthew 5:16 NAS).

This is a command from our Lord. It is not "If I feel like it," or
"When I get around to it." Since He paid the ultimate price for our

salvation and our obedience, He needs us to spread the word of His offer of salvation.

CRUMBS FROM HIS TABLE: THE BUSH I HAVE SPOKEN OF WAS NOT LIKE MOSES' BURNING BUSH, BUT WE MUST HAVE A "BURNING" DESIRE TO TAKE OUR STORY OF CHRIST TO OTHERS WHO ARE LOST.

Looking At The Lamb

WRITTEN BY: ANDREW JAMES WOODDELL
AGE: THIRTEEN

The contented lamb is looking at his master's loving face while he is embraced in safe arms. The lamb represents me and the shepherd, being Jesus, saves me from my sin. Jesus died just to save me and then forgive me. He looks upon the lamb with a happy and bright heart. Jesus is happy I have returned, and we have to tell people about Jesus.

Looking Up

SCRIPTURE: MATTHEW 17:8 (NAS)

*"And lifting up their eyes, they saw no one,
except Jesus Himself alone."*

At the close of our morning worship service, as we were singing a beautiful, meaningful hymn which told us to keep our eyes on Jesus, I began to explore just what the words meant.

What happens to me when I keep my eyes set on Him? The pressures and troubles around me begin to fade away and not seem so troublesome. If I take my eyes off of Him, the world will come back into focus.

As Christ Followers, we must be in this world and participate in many ways of everyday life. We know that the problems we face every day, whether they are personal or around our state or nation, are formidable. If we try facing them without the help and leadership of Jesus, we will fail miserably.

However, when we focus on Him and keep looking at that beautiful face, the light that shines from Him will blind us to the world problems and lead us through. But we MUST keep our spiritual eyes focused on Him.

A CRUMB FROM HIS TABLE: AS THE SCRIPTURE SAYS, "…TO SEE NO ONE EXCEPT JESUS HIMSELF ALONE IS TO NEED NO ONE ELSE BUT JESUS HIMSELF ALONE," (MATTHEW 17:8 NAS).

Magnificent Presence

SCRIPTURE: PSALM 139:7 (KJV)

"Whither shall I go from Thy Spirit? Or whither shall I flee from Thy presence?"

Magnificent: grand, glorious, lavish, sublime, exalted.

Presence: existence in a certain place, nearness, immediate vicinity, appearance.

I was looking through a catalog one evening and saw a book advertised with the word "magnificent" in its title. Immediately, the words, "Magnificent Presence," flashed into my mind; and I knew it was the Holy Spirit speaking to me. This is the first time in months that I have "heard" from Him so plainly. He has spoken to me quite often, and I have learned to listen for the message He has for me (and I hope for others).

The first thing I did was look in a dictionary for the definition of these two words. The meanings are written above. As I am writing this, I am listening to the Spirit's direction because He is the author of this letter and not I.

Let's look at the word "magnificent" and its meaning. First we have the word "grand." Grand means great. In Judges 2:7, the Scripture talks about the "great work of the Lord." We can look all around us and see God's great work. But He also works quietly in us as He sees what He knows we need from Him.

The next word is "glorious." "His glory is great in Thy salvation…" (Psalm 21:5 KJV). His (Christ's) glory was as glorious as it will ever be when He hung on that cross for us. His glory is so great that none of us can completely comprehend that thing He has done for us! Praise His Name!

We know God is generous. Look how He lavishes us with great blessings which we do not deserve. He lavishes us with His unrestrained love. He gave His Son for us, didn't He? Look around and count your blessings, seen and unseen.

We exalt His name every time we think about Him; when we pray to Him; when we sing to Him; when we read His Word; and when we are in Bible study or a worship service. He is exalted by us as we are riding down the road praising Him or just feeling His sublime arms enfolding us. "O magnify the Lord with me, and let us exalt His name together," (Psalm 34:3 KJV).

The second word, "presence," makes me want to kneel with my face on the ground before Him. I feel as though I am in His Holy Presence right now. Amen.

God's existence is in a certain place we know as heaven. Jonah 1:9 declares, "The Lord God of heaven" which describes Him as being there. But we know God is everywhere He wants to be. He is certainly not restricted to one place. These verses from the book of Psalms show His omnipresence: "If I ascend up into heaven, Thou art there; if I make my bed in hell, behold, Thou art there. If I take the wings of the morning, and dwell in the uttermost parts of the sea; even there shall Thy hand lead me, and Thy right hand shall hold me. If I say, surely the darkness shall cover me; even the night shall be light about me. Yea, the darkness hideth not from Thee;

but the night shineth as the day; the darkness and the light are both alike to Thee," (Psalm 139:8–12 KJV).

Why did the Holy Spirit put these two words together and put them in my mind? I believe it is because He wants me to dwell on God's magnificence—not just as a passing thought, but to finally realize just what a grand and glorious God I claim!

He is Lord God of heaven, the King eternal. He is incomparable, inscrutable, unchangeable, infinite, eternal, all-powerful, all-knowing, and wise. To think He is "all-everything," and yet He chooses to be in my presence as I am in His. "Who is man, that thou art mindful of him?" (Psalm 8:4 KJV). Yet You do love me and show me your "Magnificent Presence" at all times.

CRUMBS FROM HIS TABLE: YOU ARE THE "I AM" OF MY LIFE.

My Friend

He had been with me for over fifteen years and loved me unconditionally. If I was angry with him for messing up the floor, he just looked at me, adoringly. Anything I did was okay with him.

He was getting very old. According to dog years, he was at least 119, had become blind with cataracts, and was deaf. However, he still would find me wherever I was in the house—he didn't want to be far away from me.

As I sat on our back porch in the mornings, drinking my coffee, he always lay beside me. His legs had become weak, so I had to help him stand up in order for him to walk.

I remember when he was young. He used to chase squirrels up the oak tree in our back yard and would jump and bark at them as if he was going to climb the tree after them. Then, he would prance across the yard with his hair flowing, looking regal.

This special friend of mine was named Boomer. He was a black, brown, and white Sheltie and truly a beautiful dog. Everyone loved him because he was so sweet and gentle with the best disposition I've ever seen.

God certainly must love dogs because He has made so many different kinds which come in all sizes and colors. Also, I am convinced that God has given them spirits. They don't have souls, but I believe they have spirits.

All of the dogs I have had in my seventy-nine years of life have been wonderful, and I have loved them dearly. I had Pan—a German Shepherd, Ted—a German Shepherd, Sugar—a toy Spitz, April—an All-American, Daisy—a Schnauzer, Mike—the son of April, Pepper—a Peka-Scott, Val—the daughter of Pepper, Muffin—a poor waif that I adopted, and my beloved Boomer—a Sheltie.

I have had different breeds, but all were kind and gentle. I think a lot of their attitudes and dispositions come from the people they love.

If God loves us so much that He sent His only Son to die for our sins, I know He loves us enough to let our best friends' spirits be with us in heaven.

So to my best friend, Boomer, I miss you dreadfully and have shed a lot of tears as I write this. But I know I will see you again one glorious day.

Your best friend, Mama.

CRUMBS FROM HIS TABLE: THANK YOU, LORD, FOR LENDING BOOMER TO ME.

My Tribute To Sara

SCRIPTURE: JOHN 1:9 (KJV)

"That was the true Light, which lighteth every man that cometh into the world."

Her name is Sara. To be precise, her name is Sara Olive Parker Bencivenga. Sara went home with our Lord Jesus yesterday. She had been ill for quite a while, but she was reluctant to leave Andy, her husband of fifty-nine years, her two daughters, Tricia and Junie, and son, Alan.

As she began slipping away, her breathing became more difficult. Her sister, June, was at her bedside. Seeing her struggle, June said, "Go ahead, Sara, Mother is waiting for you." And she took one last breath. June said that she had just asked the Holy Spirit to come and take Sara home. In a few minutes, June's heart-breaking plea was granted.

In the Scripture above, it says that Jesus is the "Light of the World." We who love and serve Him know this. If Jesus is the Light, we who follow Him are also lights. I like to think we, Christ's Followers, are like candles compared to His Light. Our candle lights glow for Him and because of Him. He has shown His great love for us, and we hold our "candles" high for Him and for the ones we love here on earth. His followers, together, create "light" for the world which points to Jesus.

Sara is a beloved first cousin of mine and has always been as close as a sister to me. I have other "sister-cousins" I am very close to, but Sara is the first to leave me.

As I was thinking about the Light and us being candle lights, I thought about Sara's candle going out. To me the world is a little darker now, but I know her candle is blazing in heaven!

Dear Sara, I miss you so, but I know you will be there to welcome me some day when I go home. I love you.

CRUMBS FROM HIS TABLE: "YE ARE THE LIGHT OF THE WORLD…NEITHER DO MEN LIGHT A CANDLE, AND PUT IT UNDER A BUSHEL…" (MATTHEW 5:14–15 KJV).

No Ram

SCRIPTURE: GENESIS 22:13 (NAS)

"Then Abraham raised his eyes and looked, and behold, behind him a ram caught in the thicket by his horns; and Abraham went and took the ram, and offered him up for a burnt offering in the place of his son."

Oh, Lord God, You provided a ram for Abraham to sacrifice instead of his son, Isaac. But no "ram" came forth to be sacrificed in place of Your Son, Jesus.

Abraham's ram sacrifice was made for atonement for his sins. The sacrifice of Jesus Christ on the cross was God's way of atonement for our sins.

A CRUMB FROM HIS TABLE: THE OLD RUGGED CROSS IS THE DIFFERENCE.

Nothing But The Blood

SCRIPTURE: HEBREWS 9:14 (KJV)

"How much more shall the blood of Christ, who through the eternal Spirit offered Himself without spot to God, purge your conscience from dead works to serve the living God?"

There is NO wrong side of the cross. It doesn't matter to which side of the cross we come. Jesus died on the WHOLE cross. His blood was spilled over ALL of the cross, just as His blood is spilled over ALL of us when we take Him as our Lord and Savior.

It is not the cross itself that saves us, but the Son of God who died on it. He was a completely sinless man, a PERFECT lamb, who was sacrificed because of our sin. This is the plan God has for us, that we who are full of sin can become sinless through Jesus' blood sacrifice for us. His blood MUST cover us to block out all of our sin. This is the only way we are able to spend eternity with Him.

CRUMBS FROM HIS TABLE: NOTHING BUT THE BLOOD OF JESUS CHRIST CAN CLEANSE OUR SIN AWAY.

The Cabin

SCRIPTURE: EPHESIANS 1:3 (NAS)

*"Blessed be the God and Father of our Lord Jesus Christ,
who has blessed us with every spiritual blessing in the
heavenly places in Christ."*

As I sit on the porch of our cabin in the mountains of North Georgia, I hear the ever so gentle roar of the breeze as it creeps through
the tall pines. The trees sway gently as the wind passes through them
as if dancing to music that only they can hear.

My husband, Bill; daughter, Wendi; her husband, Harry; and
their son Andy are with me. We have been blessed by God in so
many ways. One of the most obvious is our cabin that He has given
us. Bill's and my dream was to have a cabin in the mountains on an
acre of land with a creek nearby. Thankfully, God fulfilled our
dream exactly as we wanted! Thank You, our Father.

As I sit on the porch, listening to the wind in the trees and feeling the gentleness of it, it makes me think of the gentleness of the
Spirit of God's love and care for me. He is always gentle and easy to
love as He listens and hears us speaking to Him. He is never loud
or harsh as He communicates with us but gentle as a summer
breeze.

We have dedicated our cabin to God and have asked Him to give all who stay in it peace and blessings.

Thank You, Lord, for Your many blessings and especially for our little piece of heaven on earth, our cabin.

CRUMBS FROM HIS TABLE: WE COULD NEVER OUT-GIVE YOU, MY LORD.

Our Constant Lord

SCRIPTURE: PHILIPPIANS 3:13–14 (KJV)

"Brethren, I count not myself to have apprehended: but this one thing I do, forgetting those things which are behind, and reaching forth unto those things which are before, I press toward the mark for the prize of the high calling of God in Christ Jesus."

One Sunday morning in the worship service, we were singing a song about our ground being holy. When our congregation sings these worship choruses, I usually close my eyes and feel the presence of the Lord. This is what I was doing this particular morning.

Suddenly, God gave me this wondrous vision: I saw Jesus walking around through the people and loving them. He, somehow, was putting His arms around us all. Then, He was standing in front of the congregation with His arms outstretched as if to encompass us all at once. The features that struck me the most were His beautiful eyes and face. I cannot describe them because I do not know any words that can. Then as I looked at Him, I saw angels standing up and down the aisles of the sanctuary. No, they didn't have wings. They were very tall and big and were dressed in tan and brown tunic type shirts and pants.

The vision lasted only a few seconds, and I could see it no more. I was so awed and humbled that I could only cry silent tears and couldn't understand why I was given this great gift. What was I supposed to do with it? Should I tell others? What did the vision mean? I asked the Lord to give me the answer if He wanted me to know.

I believe that He gave me the answer a few weeks later.

About a month after the vision, our church family received a set of blows. First, our beloved pastor of seventeen years, Dr. Don Maiden, told us he felt God had told him he would no longer be our pastor. Then, a week later, our assistant pastor, Jimmy Hallford, whom we also loved, and whom had been with us about seventeen years, was also going to leave to go be a pastor in another church. As a result, our church family would be in a grieving process for a while.

I think the Lord gave me the vision because He knew what was going to happen in our church life in a few weeks, and He wanted us to know we are still His people who have been faithful to Him. He controls our future, and He and His angels would continue to watch over us and guide us where He wants us to go. We can only follow Him, knowing He knows what lies ahead of us. He has not led us this far to abandon us now.

A CRUMB FROM HIS TABLE: THANK YOU LORD, THAT YOU ARE THE ONE CONSTANT IN OUR LIVES. EVERYTHING AND EVERYONE AROUND US MAY CHANGE, BUT YOU WILL ALWAYS BE THE SAME.

Outside The Gate

SCRIPTURE: HEBREWS 13:12 (NAS)

"Therefore Jesus also, that He might sanctify the people through His own blood, suffered outside the gate."

In Old Testament times, the sacrifice was burned outside the camp of the Israelites. "For the bodies of those animals…are burned outside the camp," (Hebrews 13:11 NAS). When Jesus died on the cross, He died "outside the gate" of the city.

Why was the sacrifice and Jesus' death completed outside the gate? Inside the camp and inside the city represent the world where we live in. It is an immoral, wicked, sinful place in which we have to live. While we are living here, we are constantly seeking something that will satisfy an empty place in us.

When we see and follow Jesus as He carries the cross outside the city gates, we begin to understand what we have been seeking. Then the Holy Spirit reveals to us the reason we see Jesus die on the cross, and we learn that it is to make us free in Him.

We realize now why He died outside the gate. We have to live in the city (or sinful world); however, we no longer are of the world. We now are "of" Jesus and belong to Him and His "world." We are now waiting and looking for the "New City" which He has promised us and will be safe for us "inside the gate."

A CRUMB FROM HIS TABLE: "LOOK UP FOR YOUR REDEMPTION DRAWS NIGH," (LUKE 21:28).

Reject Him?
Not Me, Lord!

SCRIPTURE: JOHN 18:25 (KJV)

"And Simon Peter stood and warmed himself. They said therefore unto him, 'Art not thou also one of His disciples?' He denied it, and said, 'I am not.'"

Peter denied Jesus three times because of FEAR! He was afraid for his life.

When we deny Jesus when He wants us to serve Him in a place where He is working, we deny Him out of fear. We are afraid we may fail because we aren't equipped to serve in what He is asking us to do. When we refuse to do His work, we are rejecting Him. Whatever Jesus asks us to do, He will always equip us for it. We must depend on the Holy Spirit to instruct us in what and how to do the service Christ has assigned us. We cannot fail in our service to Him when we depend on the Spirit, but we will fail Him and ourselves when we try to do everything by ourselves.

A CRUMB FROM HIS TABLE: SUBMIT OUR WILL TO HIS WILL EVERY DAY. WE RECEIVE GOD'S FAITH BY OBEDIENCE.

Set Free

SCRIPTURE: JOHN 8:36 (NAS)
*"If therefore the Son shall make you free,
you shall be free indeed."*

When Jesus sets you free, you are free indeed! Being free, as Jesus frees me, means I am free to worship Him as it pleases Him and me. It means I'm free from old restraints, habits, order of worship, and rituals that have inhibited me in worshiping Him as He deserves. I don't apologize to anyone for raising my hands in worship to Him, in praising Him with my lips and voice, even shouting, "Alleluia, praise the Lord, I love you, Jesus!" when the Spirit bids me.

This is what freedom is all about!

I had never known what worship experience I could have with a beautiful chorus we sing. Being filled with the Holy Spirit has made my worship of my Lord freer. I'm free and able to receive in my spirit the joy of the Holy Spirit. Just think, I can have this wondrous, joyful experience every time I sing, read Scripture, or just hear a beautiful song about my Lord!

Lord Jesus, thank You for setting me free from the shackles of "how we used to worship when I was young, or what my parents and grandparents used to do in church." No wonder I was bored to tears in church! I wasn't bored with Jesus; I just never had anyone tell or show me how much FUN worshiping Him could be.

Thank You, Lord. Praise Your name, the name above all names. Come and join me in some FUN!

CRUMBS FROM HIS TABLE: "SHOUT JOYFULLY TO THE LORD, ALL THE EARTH. SERVE THE LORD WITH GLADNESS; COME BEFORE HIM WITH JOYFUL SINGING. ENTER HIS GATES WITH THANKSGIVING AND HIS COURTS WITH PRAISE. GIVE THANKS TO HIM; BLESS HIS NAME, (PSALM 100:1–2, 4 NAS).

Sin's Price

SCRIPTURE: 2 CORINTHIANS 5:21 (KJV)

*"For He hath made Him to be sin for us, who knew no sin;
that we might be made the righteousness of God in Him."*

The only one God ever turned His face away from was His own Son, Jesus Christ. That was because Jesus was covered with EVERY sin that the world would ever know. God cannot look upon sin! He could look on Jesus again only after the price for sin was paid.

On the cross, Jesus cries out, "My God, My God, why hast Thou forsaken Me?" (Mark 15:34 NAS). For the first time, Christ knew He was completely alone without His loving Father or the Holy Spirit. But He also knew this was the Father's plan to salvage His lost children and that He would soon be with the Father.

CRUMBS FROM HIS TABLE: WHAT WILL YOU DO WITH JESUS? THERE IS NO GRAY AREA WITH HIM. YOU EITHER ACCEPT HIM AS SAVIOR, OR YOU DON'T ACCEPT HIM. SOMEDAY YOU MAY BE ASKING WHAT HE WILL DO WITH YOU.

Stairway

"And he (Jacob) came to a certain place and spent the night there, because the sun had set; and he took one of the stones of the place and put it under his head, and lay down in that place. And he had a dream, and behold a ladder was set on the earth with its top reaching to heaven; and behold, the angels of God were ascending and descending on it."

In an old country store in Sautee, Georgia, are many nineteenth and twentieth century goods that were once sold there. It must have been a two-story building at one time because there is a staircase that ends at the ceiling—a stairway that goes nowhere.

I was thinking about that stairway today and began comparing it to life. How easy it is to spend life going, constantly going, but not getting anywhere. It's like the old saying about a ship without a rudder. It floats around but never goes anywhere.

Life without Jesus is like that stairway. We work hard, trying to afford what this world offers. When we get what we have strived for so hard, we find out it didn't "lead anywhere," only to a desire for something else. The things this world offers are only temporary at best. The joy of obtaining "things" doesn't last long.

When God formed us, He set aside a small place in our being that nothing else can fill but Him. Try as we might, nothing will ever take away this feeling that we are not quite complete. All of the

99

homes, cars, clothes, jewels, boats, vacation homes, education, big companies, and wealth will never fill that special place. Only the Holy Spirit can fill it, and He can only fill it with our Lord Jesus. We have to ask Him to come into our hearts because He won't come in unasked.

Stop trying to walk up the stairs that go nowhere and start up the stairs that lead to more than we could ever imagine. The treasure that God has for us cannot be bought by us. You see, Jesus has bought it for us; the gift has been paid for in full to all who will believe in Him as God's only Son.

The wonderful thing about trusting in Jesus is we get rewards right away as well as our rewards which we get in heaven. Nothing can fill our hearts with pure joy the way He can. Just to say His name, "Jesus," fills us with such love and excitement that we can hardly contain ourselves.

So, come on, get off the stairs to nowhere, and join me on the stairs to the most important place—God's heaven!

CRUMBS FROM HIS TABLE: WHAT A DAY OF REJOICING WHEN WE CLIMB THAT STAIRWAY TO HEAVEN AND SEE JESUS!

Tears On My Feet

SCRIPTURE: LUKE 7:38 (NAS)

"And standing behind Him (Jesus) at His feet, weeping, she began to wet His feet with her tears..."

Have you ever had anyone's tears fall on your feet? I never had until one day.

I have prayed many intercessory prayers for people who were physically or emotionally ill, as well as for our state, nation, and churches. Most people for whom I have prayed have wept and I along with them. There is something about holding someone's hand as you pray for them that seems to join you both together with the Lord. You can actually feel the love coming from the Lord through you into that person.

So it happened when I was praying for a special person and friend. She was a new Christian and loved Jesus, but I believe that Satan was attacking her through her husband.

This day she was very upset and crying. I asked if I could pray for her, and she was eager for me to do so. Therefore, we went into a secluded place to pray.

We were standing, and I took hold of her hands. As I was

praying, I felt something soft drop on my foot but didn't pay much attention to it and kept praying. In a few moments, I felt it again and soon felt a few more drops. Then I realized it was her tears falling on my feet! Such a feeling of humbleness went through me that I cannot describe. She then looked into my eyes with the most beautiful and indescribable look I have ever seen. That look and the feeling of those tears are indelible in my mind. Many times, I have pondered on what that indescribable look could have meant. I think the Holy Spirit is giving me the answer as I write this. I believe her eyes, at that moment in time, were the eyes of Jesus, looking at me with HIS kind of love, agape love. I believe that is what this person was feeling for me at that moment, agape love—God's love!

Oh, that everyone could have the great blessing of someone's tears on their feet.

A CRUMB FROM HIS TABLE: "MISERY WEEPS AT THE FEET OF MERCY."

P.S. When you are with someone and the Spirit moves you to pray for that person, do it right then. You (or that person) may not know why the prayer is needed, but God knows.

The Answer

SCRIPTURE: I JOHN 2:17 (KJV)

"....but he that doeth the will of God abideth for ever."

SCRIPTURE: 2 CHRONICLES 7:14 (KJV)

"If My people, which are called by My name, shall humble themselves, and pray, and seek My face, and turn from their wicked ways; then will I hear from heaven, and will forgive their sin, and will heal their land."

If I could snap my fingers and know I couldn't fail, what would I do? I would tell all the people in our United States that the reason we have such moral decay, crimes of all kind, enmity between races, abortion, and everything else that is cursing our nation today, is that we are disobeying God's commandments. The Bible has the perfect solution to those problems. It is very simple. Start reading the Word of God—the Bible, accept Jesus as our Savior, and trust in Him and pray. He will deliver us and restore our nation as He promised in 2 Chronicles 7:14.

If you were to go talk to a group of my friends, what would they say I am really interested in or passionate about? I would hope they would say that I am interested in and passionate about my Lord, my family, lost people, my church and my country.

In 2 Chronicles 7:14, God tells us that if we turn from our wicked ways, humble ourselves to Him and seek Him, He will hear our prayers, forgive our sins, and heal our land.

CRUMBS FROM HIS TABLE: ASK GOD WHAT HE WANTS, NOT WHAT YOU WANT.

The Butterfly

SCRIPTURE: 2 CORINTHIANS 6:2 (NAS)
*"…behold, now is The ACCEPTABLE TIME, behold,
now is THE DAY OF SALVATION."*

I was sitting on the porch of our cabin in the mountains of North Georgia, enjoying the beauty our God has given us. Suddenly, I saw a butterfly lying on the ground, so I picked it up and took it with me back to the porch.

As I looked at how beautiful and intricately it was made, I wondered how anyone can doubt there is God. (Not "a god" but GOD, our Heavenly Creator.) I thought about the process this butterfly went through to become such a perfect, marvelous creation.

It was a lowly worm whose whole existence was eating; then it became a worm inside a cocoon. It stayed in the cocoon the allotted time God gave it to transform into the next stage in its life. Finally, the time came when it was "called" forth from its prison. God completely transformed it into one of His most beautiful creatures.

You know, God does this for us.

We begin as just a small speck and are "cocooned" in the womb for a while. Then in the fullness of God's timing we begin the next stage of our lives. We are just babes, wanting to do nothing but to satisfy our own selfish whims.

We can grow into adulthood this way if we do not try to find and fill the space in ourselves which God left in us when we were formed. This space is the "hunger and thirst" after God hole in our hearts, and only He and the Holy Spirit can fill it.

God didn't create a space like this in the butterfly. He didn't need to. The butterfly is perfect already and didn't have to have salvation. However, we are made to be like God, but because of our sin nature, we are not perfect. Therefore, we are separated from fellowship with Him.

He had to make a way for us to be "perfect" in His sight. The only way we can be seen as perfect in His sight is to be covered with the blood from His sacrificial Lamb, Jesus Christ. The choice is ours: covered with the precious blood or filthy with sin.

Personally, I want God to be able to see me "perfect."

God gives us, like the butterfly, an allotted time He wants us to be saved through the blood of His Son, but He will not give us forever to accept it.

CRUMBS FROM HIS TABLE: HE HAS TOLD US "…NOW IS THE DAY OF SALVATION" (2 CORINTHIANS 6:2 NAS). IF GOD IS POWERFUL ENOUGH TO CREATE A BEAUTIFUL BUTTERFLY, HE IS POWERFUL ENOUGH TO CREATE IN US A NEW, BORN-AGAIN LIFE TO LIVE FOR HIM.

The Cross

SCRIPTURE: I CORINTHIANS 1:18 (NAS)

"For the word of the cross is to those who are perishing foolishness, but to us who are being saved it is the power of God."

Look at the cross on which Jesus died. Do you see four points to it? One points to heaven, two and three point to east and west or north and south, depending on the direction it is turned. The fourth points downward, as if pointing to hell. Jesus died on this cross to point us to heaven and eternal life with Him.

The arms of the cross, like the arms of Jesus, are outstretched to encompass the whole world. His feet, or the foot of the cross, shows the direction we, and the rest of the world, will go if we do not believe in His dying for us to remove our sins. He proved His great gift of forgiveness and our eternal life with Him when He rose from the grave!

PRAISE GOD!
THANK YOU, JESUS!

CRUMBS FROM HIS TABLE: JESUS WAITED TO DIE UNTIL THE LAST PERSON

ON EARTH WOULD BE SAVED WHO WAS TO BE SAVED. THEN HE COULD SAY, "IT IS FINISHED."

The Eyes Of God

SCRIPTURE: 2 CHRONICLES 16:9A (KJV)

"For the eyes of the Lord run to and fro throughout the whole earth, to shew Himself strong in the behalf of them whose heart is perfect toward Him…"

Some years ago, when I was asked to teach an adult ladies' Sunday School class, I felt there was no way I was qualified to do this. Our former teacher was very knowledgeable of God's Word, and we adored her. I could see no way that I would ever measure up to her teaching. Reluctantly, I accepted the position but was really insecure. For a year, I anguished over teaching this class and kept apologizing for my shortcomings because I knew I wasn't teaching like Sarah.

I wish I had known the above verse sooner. It would have relieved a lot of grief on my part. Even though I knew that God was with me and had "something" to do with bringing this job to me, I wouldn't be quiet and listen for His orders because I was too busy feeling inadequate and a bit overwhelmed.

One day, He finally got my attention. He told me it didn't matter if I felt inferior, that He wasn't. He chose me because I was a blank page on which He could write the things He wanted to write. The only thing I had to do was to give my whole life over to Him and not try to hold on to a part of it. I was to give "every" Sunday School lesson over to Him to write it as He pleased. I wasn't to worry about what I was going to say. That is entirely up to Him and the Holy Spirit. He just wanted me to write and teach the words He gave to me.

I have done what He commanded, and my worries and fears have evaporated like steam. If I ever try to write a lesson without Him, I am a complete failure. I thank my Lord for not giving up on me.

The verses I am studying today are ones I should get to know in my heart. He says, "My grace is sufficient for you, for power is perfected in weakness," (2 Corinthians 12:9–10 NAS). Of course His grace is sufficient! Why didn't I see that right away? Because I had let myself get between Him and me. Now I know that because of my weakness, "My strength is made perfect."

Because of His strength He can make me strong! It is great to know the Lord God is looking constantly for someone He can help. As the Scripture says, "The eyes of the Lord move to and fro." I am so glad that His eyes were (are) upon me. All that I am or ever will be is because of my Lord.

CRUMBS FROM HIS TABLE: LORD, THANK YOU FOR SEEING ME AND KNOWING THE HELP I NEEDED (THEN AND NOW.) HELP ME TO BE AWARE OF THE GREAT PROMISES YOU GIVE TO ME. HELP ME NEVER TO LET MYSELF COME BETWEEN YOU AND ME. I LOVE YOU, LORD.

The Gift That Gives

Today is Easter Sunday, one of the most sacred days in our Baptist faith. As Christ Followers we rejoice over this day that represents the day our Lord rose from His grave, just as He promised.

We know about His triumphal entrance into Jerusalem and how the people showered Him with praise and adoration. This wonderful welcome for Jesus would soon turn into a shouting, angry mob that cried, "Crucify Him! Crucify Him!"

In His short ministry, Jesus had told His disciples He was the Son of God. "And the Word became flesh, and dwelt among us, and we beheld His glory, glory as of the only begotten from the Father, full of grace and truth," (John 1:14 NAS). He also said that He came as a "shepherd" to guide and protect His "sheep." We are His sheep, and He knows us and we know "His voice." He would lay down His life for His sheep. "For the Son of Man has come to seek and to save that which was lost" (Luke 19:10 NAS).

Nothing in these Scripture verses are new to us. Most of us have heard them taught over and over. Sometimes we can read verses so much that, unless we stop and listen to what we are reading, they become just words on a page. May it never be, Lord, when I read Your Holy Scripture!

Just as Jesus told Thomas, "…Blessed are they who did not see, and yet believed" (John 20:29 NAS). Think how much Jesus loves us because we accept Him in faith and not by sight. Years ago a pastor in our church was preaching on faith and said, "Believing is seeing." How good those words are. When we believe in Christ, He shows things to us we never could see before we were saved. If we listen, really listen, He will speak to us in many ways. We have to tune in to Him and get on His wave length. We can do this by reading His word and quietly meditating on it.

Jesus gave His life so that we could have life. "And He said to them, 'Thus it is written, that the Christ should suffer and rise again from the dead the third day,'" (Luke 24:46 NAS).

His resurrection is predicted in several places in the Old Testament. "For thou wilt not abandon my soul to Sheol; neither wilt Thou allow Thy Holy One to undergo decay," (Psalms 16:10 NAS). "But the Lord was pleased to crush Him, putting Him to grief; if He would render Himself as a guilt offering…" (Isaiah 53:10 NAS). And in Acts 13:35, "Therefore He also says in another Psalm, 'THOU WILT NOT ALLOW THY HOLY ONE TO UNDERGO DECAY.'"

Without our faith in Jesus Christ, we cannot please Him. Our Savior is the driving force behind all that we do in His name. We are spinning our wheels in Florida sand if we try doing anything without the faith that comes from knowing Him. He rewards us for our faith in Him (Hebrews 11:6).

He does not give help to angels but to us, the descendants of Abraham. Because we are not Jewish, we are "grafted" into the family that God began in Abraham.

After His death and resurrection, Christ had a new life and body.

He had completed His assignment from God and was pleasing to Him.

Our new life comes after we have accepted Christ's death as payment for our old sinful life. Our Father, God, is pleased with us.

Before Jesus ascended into heaven, He promised to send "forth the promise of My Father upon you," (Luke 24:49). This promise that God sent was the Holy Spirit. Thank You, Lord, for this wonderful gift! He abides in believers today.

CRUMBS FROM HIS TABLE: CHRIST GAVE US THE GREAT GIFT OF SALVATION. IT IS THE GIFT THAT GIVES!

The Light
And The Lamp

SCRIPTURE: PSALM 119:105 (NAS)
"Thy Word is a lamp to my feet, and a light to my path."

This is a beautiful way of showing God's watchful eye on us.

First, His Word is a "lamp to our feet." When we are in His Word daily, it is as if a lamp is shining on our steps as we start our day. He continually shines that lamp so we don't stumble over obstacles put in our way. How wonderful to know God controls the lamp and will never put it out as long as we depend on Him and His Word.

Second, there is "the light to my path." The light differs from the lamp in that it shines on the path ahead of us.

God holds the light so we won't stumble along our way. The light is like a map. It shows what is in our path so that we can avoid the pitfalls of the evil one.

One way God protects us is by keeping the light on our path so we will see the way He leads us.

CRUMBS FROM HIS TABLE: AS WE STUDY HIS WORD AND STAY CLOSE TO HIM, WE FIND A GREAT TRUTH. GOD IS THE LIGHT!

The Mourning, Morning Star

SCRIPTURE: REVELATION 22:16 (NAS)

"I, Jesus, have sent My angel to testify to you these things for the churches. I am the root and the offspring of David, the bright morning star."

In Revelation 22:16, Jesus describes Himself as "the bright morning star." There are other Scripture references to the "morning star." 2 Peter 1:19 says in part "…until the day dawns and the morning star arises in your hearts." Also in Revelation 2:28 Jesus said, "I will give him the morning star."

We, as Christ Followers, know Jesus as our "bright morning star." He has revealed this to us in His Word.

As we begin our journey with Him, He is the light that shines in the darkness of unbelief and turns our "night of unbelief" into the dawn of understanding who He is. Just before dawn breaks each day, the morning star shines brightest. It's the same way with our "dawn" into the day Christ leads us. He is always here for us, no matter what "time of day" it is.

I was thinking about Christ, the morning star, and I wondered if He is also Christ, the "mourning" star? The Scripture speaks of God wiping away tears in Isaiah 25:8. According to Revelation

21:4, God finally wipes away "every tear from their eyes" in the New Heaven and New Earth.

I wonder if Christ mourns for those whom He died to set free from sin? I'm sure He mourns for those who have heard about the sins He bore for them on the cross, but don't seem to care. They go on with their lives, blaspheming His marvelous name in many ways. They never care that the Creator of the universe, God's Son, Creator of man, Creator of an everlasting, perfect life with Him forever, is mourning for them. Just as we mourn for our children who go astray, how much more Christ must mourn for His lost children. We do not understand the kind of grief He has any more than we understand that kind of love He has for us.

I know "Jesus wept" (John 11:35) while here on earth. Does He weep and mourn today for those who reject His great gift and Him? Knowing Him as the Good Shepherd, I think He does.

CRUMBS FROM HIS TABLE: OF THIS I AM SURE; THERE WILL BE NO WEEPING OR MOURNING FOR US WHEN WE ARE WITH CHRIST FOREVER IN THE NEW HEAVEN AND NEW EARTH! (REVELATION 21:4).

The One Who Spoke

SCRIPTURE: JOHN 1:1–3 (NAS)

"In the beginning was the Word, and the Word was with God, and the Word was God. He was in the beginning with God. All things came into being by Him, and apart from Him nothing came into being that has come into being."

This Scripture reminds me of an evening at our church (Northridge Church, Haines City, Florida) when our former pastor, Dr. Don Maiden, was leading a Bible study. He was talking about Jesus and the Holy Spirit being in us when we are truly born again. He was saying how the Spirit speaks to us and for us. Our advocate before God is Jesus Christ, who prays on our behalf before God.

The Bible says in Luke 22:31–32, "Simon, Simon, behold Satan has demanded permission to sift you like wheat; but I have prayed for you, that your faith may not fail; and you, when once you have turned again, strengthen your brothers."

Dr. Maiden continued on to tell that Jesus (the Word) was the One who "spoke" into being the universe. Just then the Holy Spirit spoke to me these words. "The One who 'spoke' into being the earth and the universes is the same One who speaks to you." This revelation from the Spirit humbled me so that I wanted to fall on my knees.

This was just one more confirmation from my Lord to let me know how important all of His people are to Him, including myself!

Thank You, my Lord, for Your great love!!

CRUMBS FROM HIS TABLE: WHAT LOVE HE HAS FOR US, THAT HE, THE CREATOR OF THIS WORLD AND EVERYTHING IN IT, KNOWS US BY NAME! AND HE PRAYS FOR US BY NAME!

The Real
Meaning Of Easter

What is the real meaning of Easter to you? Is it Easter bunnies, egg hunts, new clothes, and candy, or something else?

This Sunday, we celebrate the resurrection of our Lord and Savior, Jesus Christ, Easter. God forbid that we treat this most sacred of days as just another Sunday.

We read the story of His betrayal, trials, persecution, and death from the Gospels each year; so we are familiar with it. I started to write this and looked at Matthew, Mark, Luke, and John to review the facts; however, the Holy Spirit led me to Isaiah: "He was despised and forsaken of men, a man of sorrows, and acquainted with grief; and like one from whom men hide their face, He was despised, and we did not esteem Him," (Isaiah 53:3–6 NAS).

"Surely our griefs (sickness) He Himself bore, and our sorrows He carried; yet we ourselves esteemed Him stricken, smitten of God, and afflicted.

"But He was pierced (wounded) through for our transgressions,

He was crushed for our iniquities; the chastening for our well being fell upon Him, and by His scourging (stripes) we are healed.

"All of us like sheep have gone astray, each of us has turned to his own way; but the Lord has caused the iniquity of us all to fall on Him," (Isaiah 54:4–6 NAS).

Isaiah wrote about "the man of sorrows" some 700 years before the birth of that man, Jesus. Isaiah was truly inspired by the Holy Spirit to be able to write about the Messiah whom he knew nothing about personally.

He was accurate when he wrote how despised this man would be. Jesus was not just despised in His day but look how people despise Him today.

The lost people of our world will do about anything to discredit Him as the savior of their future and make Him out to be just another man. We, as Christ Followers, must stand up for Him. If we fail Him, the world is lost!

We must honor Him every day because He and He alone carried our sins to that cross to be "nailed" on Him. Those horrible sins of mine and yours that he bore were more painful to Him than the nails in His hands and feet. But He became this "sin-carrier" because He loves us with a love no one can understand.

Halleluiah! I am His!

We are healed by "His scourging (stripes)." Our sin nature is under control, and our sickness in body and spirit is healed. What a great promise!

When we love Jesus with our whole being, body, soul, and spirit, we are at peace. Not the peace the world offers, but that peace that passes all understanding. "For He Himself is our peace," (Ephesians 2:14). Do you have His peace?

Thank You, Lord Jesus, for giving to us the real meaning of Easter.

The Reply

SCRIPTURE: MATTHEW 12:45 (KJV)
"Then goeth he, and taketh with himself seven other spirits more wicked than himself, and they enter in and dwell there..."

One Sunday morning as I was teaching my ladies' Bible class, one of the women asked, "Could you tell me why so many foreign religions are taking hold in America? Religions such as Islam, Buddhism, and others like them?"

I silently asked the Holy Spirit for His reply.

In Matthew 12:43–45, Jesus says that when an unclean (evil) spirit leaves a man, if the space they vacated is not filled with Jesus and the Holy Spirit, the evil spirits will return with seven more spirits than before.

In America, man has taken God out of nearly everything he can. When God is taken out of our nation, our nation is then left vulnerable to any evil religions and cults to come in and possess our people.

We must pray fervently that our nation will return to God Almighty as He founded it.

A CRUMB FROM HIS TABLE: "…AND MY PEOPLE WHO ARE CALLED BY MY NAME, HUMBLE THEMSELVES AND PRAY, AND SEEK MY FACE AND TURN FROM THEIR WICKED WAYS, THEN I WILL HEAR FROM HEAVEN, WILL FORGIVE THEIR SIN, AND WILL HEAL THEIR LAND," (2 CHRONICLES 7:14 NAS).

The Sweetest Words

SCRIPTURE: MATTHEW 25:21 (KJV)
*"His lord said unto him, 'Well done,
thou good and faithful servant."*

The sweetest words I can hear,
When before my Lord I appear,
Can only be heard in heaven above
From the One who is the Creator of love;
Oh, my Lord, to hear You say,
"Well done, my good and faithful servant,"
Will be my reward on that great day.
I could have no greater reward
Than knowing I have pleased my Lord.

A CRUMB FROM HIS TABLE: I AM SATISFIED WITH JESUS. IS JESUS SATISFIED WITH ME?

Wash His Feet

SCRIPTURE: JOHN 13:5 (NAS)

*"Then He poured water into the basin, and
began to wash the disciples' feet...."*

On the night of the Lord's Supper, the disciples and Jesus went up into the upper room. The custom of the day was to have a basin of water and a towel so that a servant could wash the feet of a guest as he entered the house. Because they wore sandals and traveled by foot, their feet were always dirty.

On this night of the Lord's Supper, no servant was there to wash the disciples' or Jesus' feet. And none of the disciples offered to wash the feet of the others. No one even offered to wash the feet of Jesus!

When I saw this statement in a book that I was reading, it really made me stop and look into my heart. Would I have washed Jesus' feet? Or would I think it was not my job but the job of a servant?

Who am I anyway? If I love Christ and seek to do His will, aren't I supposed to be a servant to others? If I don't serve others, I cannot be a servant to Jesus.

Jesus showed He was a servant to mankind when He washed the

feet of the disciples that night. Jesus is the example I am to pattern my life after. He was the greatest servant there has ever been. I cannot possibly walk in His footsteps, but I can walk as close to Him as possible. His greatest act as a servant to mankind was to die on the cross to save us from our sin so that we can spend eternity with Him.

A CRUMB FROM HIS TABLE: LORD, LET ME WASH YOUR FEET TODAY AND EVERY DAY, BY BEING A SERVANT FOR YOU TO OTHERS. I HAVE MISSED THE OPPORTUNITY MANY TIMES TO WASH YOUR FEET.

What A Savior!

SCRIPTURE: MATTHEW 28:19 (NAS)

*"Go therefore and make disciples of all nations,
baptizing them in the name of the Father and the Son
and the Holy Spirit."*

One Sunday evening, as my pastor, Dr. Don Maiden, was teaching about the Holy Spirit and the Trinity, the Holy Spirit spoke a message to my heart. This is what He said, "You get Three for the price of One. Jesus paid the price on the cross so that you can have the Father, the Son, and the Holy Spirit." God gave His only Son to pay the price for us, but He gave us a bargain. Can you imagine the magnitude of the most precious gifts?

All anyone has to do to get "Three for the price of One" is to accept Jesus as their Savior; accept Him as God's Son, crucified and resurrected for our sins. He has already PAID THE PRICE IN FULL. What a Savior!!!

CRUMBS FROM HIS TABLE: GOD IS IN THREE PERSONS, HIS BLESSED TRINITY.

Who Is This Baby?

SCRIPTURE: LUKE 1:30 (NAS)

"And behold, you (Mary) will conceive in your womb, and bear a son, and you shall name Him Jesus."

He was born in a lowly manger,
His mother a humble girl.
To some He was but a stranger,
To all the Savior of the world.
He grew up as a carpenter's son,
Just a boy who loved to pray;
His mother knew He was the One,
Who would be the Savior one day.
His ministry here on earth was short;
He taught, He healed, He shared.
He traveled the land on foot and by boat
And showed the people He cared.
Who was this Man who came to earth
And was born in a lowly way?
The Man who loved us before His birth,
He died alone that dark day.

His name is Savior, Cornerstone, Counselor,
Deliverer, Faithful and True,
First-born, First fruits, Teacher,
Messiah, King of the Jews.
But the name I love best is Jesus Christ, my Lord.

CRUMBS FROM HIS TABLE: JESUS WAS BORN IN A LOWLY MANGER, TO DIE ON A LONELY CROSS.

Who Knows Better?

SCRIPTURE: EXODUS 20:8
"Remember the sabbath day, to keep it holy."

We work seven days a week and never seem to get ahead spiritually, physically, or mentally. Why is that so? The only thing we get is further in debt and so tired we can never seem to get enough rest. So what do we do? We try to find the perfect recreation to help us get some rest. However, the only thing we get is "burn out" on every type of recreation we happen to be in at the time. Boats, planes, cars, golf, tennis, football, or recreational vehicles don't seem to appease us long. What is wrong?

In God's Ten Commandments (Exodus 20), we are commanded (NOT SUGGESTED) to work six days and rest on the seventh. We used to obey this command, but we have gradually turned the Sabbath day into just another work day. So now we choose to be without our day of rest that renews our strength and energy.

Don't you think that God knew enough about our bodies, which He designed and made, that He knew we would need a day to rest? Not a day for recreation, but a day for REST.

So many times we think we know better than God what is best for us, but our feeble attempts at serving ourselves usually fall far short of what God knows is best for us. God lets us go on in our self-deception until we find out that when we listen to Him and His commandments, we come out winners every time.

A CRUMB FROM HIS TABLE: SIX DAYS YOU ARE TO WORK, BUT ON THE SEVENTH DAY YOU SHALL CEASE FROM YOUR LABOR SO YOU MAY REFRESH YOURSELVES.

Crumbles

SCRIPTURE: LUKE 15:5 (KJV)

*"And when he hath found it, he layeth
it on His shoulders, rejoicing."*

The reason Jesus, the Good Shepherd, goes after the sheep that strays is so the false shepherd cannot steal them away.

SCRIPTURE 2: PETER 3:9 (KJV)

*"The Lord...is longsuffering to us-ward, not willing that any
should perish, but that all should come to repentance."*

The Lord is not slow in fulfilling His promise to come again; He does not want anyone to perish in their sin.

We must live our daily lives and in our Christian walk as if Jesus walks visibly by our side.

SCRIPTURE: JOHN 14:27 (KJV)

"...Let not your heart be troubled, neither let it be afraid."

Fear can paralyze. It distracts us from our purpose of serving the Lord. You cannot have fear in your mind and heart yet trust in Jesus at the same time. Putting trust in Christ Jesus gives us tranquility.

SCRIPTURE: PHILIPPIANS 4:3 (KJV)

"...my fellow laborers, whose names are in the book of life."

You can have your name on the church roll here on earth and not have your name in God's book in heaven, but you cannot have your name in God's book in heaven and not have your name in His Church roll here on earth.

CPSIA information can be obtained at www.ICGtesting.com
Printed in the USA
LVOW040850301011

252690LV00001B/3/P